love,
Me Too

LETA GREENE

SNOWY PEAKS

MEDIA

ISBN 978-1-942298-52-6

www.snowypeaksmedia.com

To the child that cannot speak out.
I hope this book helps you find your voice.

Foreword

I DIDN'T WANT TO WRITE this book. I never saw it coming.

"I heard you're writing another book," my friend said as she slid me a bank slip over the counter.

"Yes, it's all happening…" I tailed off, uncharacteristically quiet in my reply. Another bank teller that heard this became excited. It's cool news, right?

Here's the thing that is important you understand: I am really happy. Like loud happy. I am the lady that talks to you in the elevator. I will comment on your purchase at the store telling you, "Oh you'll like that, it's really yummy." I will compliment your hair, your cute purse. I will interact with your kid making faces at me in the restaurant, and I will make faces back. I am like sunshine in a bucket 94.7% of the time. I love people. I love people and I live my life assuming that you are good, that you like me. And yes, I know that isn't completely true, but I am surprised when someone is…well, bad. I feel kind of sticky even saying that.

I am so happy when people assume nothing bad has ever happened to me. I consider this to be one of my greatest life accomplishments. Horrid, ugly, hideous things have happened to me, but they happened. I wanted to crawl out of that darkness and live in the light. I live here in happy. Not drugged, not fake—real, maintainable happy. When I walk into a room, I light it up. It's a skill. I am not saying this to brag or speak of my power. I am just a sunbeam of happy. I love people and they love me. Do you hear the Barney song?

Anyway, back to my story. Many people at the bank know me, so when I was quiet it was not normal. One teller after another was excited to hear about the new book. The tellers, the bank manager, the other patrons who don't know me excitedly leaned in, wanting to be in on the news.

Then the question was asked, "What is the book about?"

I glanced at my friend, who had heard of the news from my Facebook feed. She knew the topic. She knew it was about to get uncomfortable. "It's on sunshine, unicorns…and sexual abuse." My face had a squint to it, seeing how the words landed. I tried to soften them with a smile. Perhaps I should have added in glitter.

But this book is not actually on glitter or unicorns, just sunshine and sexual abuse. There were a few shifts in posture as they stared back at me. Then as we all stood there in a circle, a remarkable thing happened: no one turned away. We started talking—women and men—all talking in a public place about the conversation we need to have about sexual abuse.

I left the bank that day feeling a different kind of light, the light of communication, the light of truth. We all agreed it was time to speak up, to share. It *should* be talked about. Only when we talk to each other—to our children, to our neighbors, and to society—can our children be safe. Sexual abuse lurks in the secret shadows of our culture. As the sterilizing heat of the sun's rays hits our previously hidden corners, it is time for me, time for the many victims who have entrusted me with their story, to speak up.

I am not a therapist. I am not trained how to listen and advise others, but I am a makeup artist and hundreds of women have shared their pain with me as I have taught them how to perfectly wing their eyeliner.

I am not a doctor. I cannot sew broken parts back together. I can't diagnose or prescribe, but I can recommend a path to healing that has worked for me.

I am not a police officer. I have not been trained on how to deal with or spot the signs of abuse, but I have stood on the front lines and been able to protect others because I've been there.

I am not an expert in this field due to years of study, but I am qualified because of the years I spent as a victim. I've learned from the teacher of experience.

You see that picture on the front cover of this book? Yeah, that's me. While some cool elements were added around it, nothing of that picture has been doctored. You can't Photoshop in that dead look in the eyes. I found this picture while helping my parents move. I felt that Little Leta was trying to tell me something, something so profound that I pasted it up in my office. There she hung for a few months. What was she trying to say? When this book came to be, my editor and I discussed what the cover should look like. My assistant chuckled, came over, and pointed out the obvious. As her finger hit the picture, it was obvious this was meant for the cover.

I am speaking out for the girl I was. What happened to me is not unique in any way. Others have shared their stories with me because they trust me. This is a sacred honor. I am also speaking out for the woman I am today, a happy, fulfilled, amazing life of sunshine. Sadly, no unicorns.

Little children, adult victims with broken hearts, and those that support them, you need to know that happiness is out there. No myth; real happiness can happen after the crushing weight of evil robs your innocent joy. This book is meant to give the broken in our hearts a voice.

2018 has been called the Year of the Woman. I think it's about time. A lot of the conversation so far has centered on sexual abuse, and countless victims have finally felt the support they needed to step forward. I applaud these brave souls. However, there are pieces missing from this conversation about sexual abuse that I'd like to see added in. Only then do I believe that our society can transform into something greater.

One night in January 2018, I couldn't sleep. I like my sleep, but words were demanding to be written. I'll be honest, I have terrible grammar, you don't know that because I have an amazing editor. If you follow me on Facebook then you would know I am not a writer, but I do have a gift with words. So when the words are coming, I recognize it's something I must write. I wrote a Facebook post on the #metoo movement on January 11, 2018, thinking it may help a few friends. I posted it just after 2:10 am. Then the thought came, *whoa … that's a lot to just put out there. I should probably think about this.* I took it down by 2:17 am and went to sleep. The words were written and they didn't have to be shared publicly, I told myself.

I really like to sleep. I like it a lot. In fact, it's kind of a joke at our house. My husband served four years in the military, and so it's now natural for him to wake up in the morning. But not me—never me. But early that morning, despite my lousy night of sleep, I woke with an urgent feeling to repost what I had written just a few short hours before. I pushed the feeling aside and told the interrupter of sleep that I had to pray about that kind of thing first. Go ahead and laugh with me for telling the impressions from God that I had to get God's approval first.

Going about my morning, the first message of the day on my phone was, "Why did you take that post down? My friend needs to read it." Oh, a second witness.

I read my post to my husband. He is a perfectly honest man with no flair for dramatics, just solid and analytical, and the love of my for-ever. As I read to him, I noticed him look down. When I had finished he looked up, his eyes a little wet and said, "You need to share that." I started to tell him why I shouldn't, but he brushed off my objections saying, "You know who helped you write that." It is a burden to be married to a man with such a good and obedient soul. He is usually right (except when it comes to decorating, chocolate intake, and his philosophy that exercise should be done often).

I reposted it and headed to my workout. My phone was blowing up with public comments, private messages, texts, calls. Within twelve hours there was a book deal. I have joked that day was so intense as God was working my objections, that my liver was having a spiritual experience. My *should I's?* were swept into a determination that regardless of my busy schedule with my makeup business, speaking contracts, and the awesome job of being a mom, that I was going to write this book.

It was a profoundly spiritual thing to know it was time to share, and not with just a few friends and clients as I had through the years when it felt right. It was time to speak up to the whole world. The #metoo movement is everywhere. I am all for women and men who have been objectified, sexualized, and silenced coming out and saying this is *not* okay. I am glad that our society is now entering into a conversation about consent. In the past we have showcased that in sexual conversations our girls should giggle when approached, be coy when touched, and then blamed when assaulted. In order to address the cause of assault we must recognize that when we engage in entertainment that mocks anyone for their color, sex, status, religion, or orientation, we are funding hate. Jesus said it this way when He said, "Love your neighbor as thyself." (Mark 12:31)

We must love ourselves and give love to others, but loving others doesn't require our bodies, as popular media teaches. Love requires our hearts. Love is built in trust, accountability, and truth. We cannot demand respect: we must give it. In that is our power. In giving respect, we will find #metoo to be an anthem of healing.

Before we get started in earnest, I want to state some ground rules.

First, I will not give the man that abused me the fame of sharing his name in this book. I also don't feel that he should get a pseudonym that may be shared with good people. But referring to him as the man-that-destroyed-my-innocence is a little wordy so I'm shortening it to MTDMI. It's a bit gangly, but it gets the point across.

Second, for our vocabulary here, I will refer to abusers in general as The Trespasser or the typical terms like perpetrator or abuser. I also understand that abusers can be both male and female, and victims can also be children and adults. For the sake of this book, we will alternate between him, her, women, men, boys, and girls.

Third, I promise you that happiness is achievable, but it will take a lot of hard work. I highly recommend involving a therapist, doctor, clergy, and other professional services. This book is meant to show you the path of healing that worked for me and others who have had similar experiences to mine and to offer you some tools I've found useful in my own journey to happiness, but it is not meant to replace professional assistance or to be an ultimate tool that will solve everything.

Sorry there won't be any unicorns, but the happiness and healing I've experienced isn't a myth.

Chapter 1

Laser Vision of Light

"With great power comes great responsibility."
-Voltaire

IT IS A WELL-KNOWN FACT that all superheroes were once misunderstood, perhaps bullied, or went through some great tragedy: Spiderman lost his parents and uncle; Batman witnessed a horrific tragedy; Hercules was always enduring mayhem; Wonder Woman had to leave behind her home. In the movies, we watch with almost giddy delight when the heroes discover who they really are and realize that they will no longer be the underdog. It is all very gratifying, isn't it?

Perhaps I always imagined I could be a superhero because I am a mutant. Seriously. I have a genetic mutation on my third and seventh chromosome, whole sections of DNA that have swapped places. It's called a translocation. So many little pieces must come together just right to make a human being, but sometimes little glitches happen, which create people like me, mutants. I like the idea that I am like the characters in the *X-Men* movies. However, I have yet to fling fire or walk through walls, and I have really wanted both of those skills at different times.

Maybe I always knew there was something different in my genetic coding. One of my earliest memories is standing on the edge of my family's couch, convinced that I could fly. My knees bent in anticipation, poised to jump into the air. For that moment it was so real.

I called my family members to see me perched on the couch edge— to my mom's credit, she never said we could stand like that on the couch. As I made the leap, I called out, "Super Leta!" I took off, swirling around the room and then came to land on the only safe place that could absorb such superhuman speed, the couch. We kids really beat up that couch with our flight landing, wrestling, jumping and flops. Somehow that couch never lost its umph.

Like Super Leta, each superhero story fits into a common theme: good will triumph over evil, right will win and wrong will fail. These themes fit so neatly into comic books or movie screens that we pay to be entertained by them. It's natural to want life to fit nicely like it does on screen. We all want to have a story arc and a clean resolution.

I may not have the superpowers of flight or laser vision I imagined in my early childhood, yet I do have power: real and lasting, a superpower no kryptonite can take from me, no villain can rob me of unless I allow it. It is the superpower of love.

I love me. I love my life. I love the people in my life.

Do I have challenges? Of course, but now I am able to recognize villains, and they fear me. They can see it in my eyes.

Evil, in all its ugly disguises, tried really hard to destroy me. It failed. Instead, it made me strong. It taught me to know the difference between cowardice and strength. As a child and an adolescent I thought I was the coward; but no, evil is the coward. It cowers when we see it for what it is. It is terrified of our laser vision of light.

I'm a mover and a doer, and when my feet hit the floor in the morning, I know an awesome day lies before me. I am a wife and mom, and those titles are my greatest joy in life, because those dreams felt so out of my reach as a child. Professionally, I am an international motivational speaker, getting the opportunity to travel all over the world and speak to audiences of all sizes. Seriously. People pay money to listen to me. On top of that, I'm a professional makeup artist. I make people feel good about themselves. These two careers have provided a financial blessing that was beyond my wildest dreams as a child.

Today, I am a powerhouse. But before that, I was a little girl. To say I was a "scared and sad" little girl would be an understatement. I grew up poor, by American standards, and often wore my older brothers' hand-me-down clothes. I was in a bike accident as a child that knocked out my three front teeth, leaving a wide gap in my smile, so I didn't smile often.

I didn't think I had a lot to smile about. I looked around and saw the differences. I couldn't relate to the things other kids were talking about like how to win at Pac-Man. I was worried about my safety, food, money, and other adult things. I had a handful of family members tell me I was unfortunate in my looks and personality so often that I internalized it. Their words became my own self talk.

When people say unkind things to you, it isn't about the words that are said, but what you do with them. Do you internalize them and squelch the voice of light? Do you enhance the wrongs and pains of the past? We all hurt; we then have a choice of what to do with that hurt. Satan, the ultimate super villain, wants us to feel alone. He wants us to feel hopeless and without choice. He wants us to feel we are powerless, when in truth we have more power than he does.

When I was young, I didn't think that happiness could be there for me. Happiness didn't find me, but I found it because I went looking for it.

Shame is a powerful emotion. It stops us. It is a favorite weapon of that dastardly super villain Satan because it binds us. Literally. If shame were just a knotted rope around our wrists, we could wriggle out of it and get free. But shame is more like a reinforced steel box without a door, it's so much more powerful than rope, which is why it's the number one weapon of choice for evil. When shame finds a place within our heart, it robs us of joy, it depletes our will to fight, or even go on trying. A smile becomes a mask that rings false and foreign. When we are filled with shame, destruction is beyond physical.

I broke free from the bondage of shame because of my super power of love, using the laser beam of light that cuts through the false prisons. I was able to take back control of my life. I moved from the stage of being a victim to the stage of being a survivor. The problem is that too many of us think that "survivor" is the resting place. It isn't. Survivors are people who are no longer being victimized. That means the abuse has stopped. They've lived it and they've survived it.

So everything is peachy, right?

Wrong.

Those of us who have been sexually abused know the damage it does to your soul. We know of the cracks, the giant rifts that have been created in our psyche. We understand the emotional trauma and hell we and those close to us have undergone. Like in the movies after an epic battle scene where good finally triumphs, we understand the destruction left behind will need to be rebuilt.

Survivors are often angry, and rightfully so. They will develop coping skills, for good or for bad. Some good skills I will describe throughout this book. Many survivors turn to addiction in all its varieties to dull the horrors. Survivors may need to talk about what happened, or they may not. Often, they seek justice.

These are all natural stages when moving from being a victim to being a survivor. All of these are common ways of dealing with trauma, but survival is not our end goal. We want to do more than survive, we want to thrive. We want more than to dull our senses; we want to enjoy a vibrant, rich life with all the happiness we are willing to receive.

Victims become survivors, but in order to thrive, they must enter a third stage that I call advocacy. Once we have walked the road of healing, we can turn around and help someone else find the path. You are forever changed because of the deeds, damage, or violence that was done to you, and you can never return to the person that you once were, but you can move forward to find a stronger, better person inside. That person is now an advocate. A superhero that helps to defend others! You simply can't be silent once you understand the damage that sexual abuse causes.

I invite you to look at your own life and see yourself as a superhero. I'm not recommending the outfit of bright colors and tight spandex. I am proposing the following approach.

This enemy you face, this battle you must win, is not just about what happened to you, but helping you turn into the hero you can and will become. I promise you it can happen. However, like all superheroes, you have to discover your powers in your own way. Right now you are writing your own origin story. You may not know what your super power is or how to use it, but I'm here to tell you that no one can fling the web for you, no one can teach you to take flight, and no one can force you to fight crime for a living. You have to work on those gifts and make those decisions for yourself.

Don't allow the super villain in your story to write what the rest of your life will be. Just like our superheroes, you don't just fight for you, you fight for the world, for your world and the world of girls, boys, women, and other victims who haven't yet found their power to overcome.

I have met many superheroes. Many of them contributed to this book. Some are sharing their name and others have chosen to maintain their secret identity.

In this book I will be speaking out about the source of my true super power, the one I had to work on. I discovered my super power through trial and error and brutally hard work. The reward is that I stand victorious in life. So do many of my friends. Can you imagine us posed with our feet apart, our fists confidently on our hips, and our faces alight with the glow of strength?

Real power is not gained by taking it from anyone else. You can only earn power by doing what it takes to make it a part of you. The secret is this: all superpowers are God-given, and they are already within you. No one, nothing can take away your super power. It is up to you to claim your power.

I had it right as a kid. I am Super Leta! So are you! Now repeat after me, "I am Super (insert name)." If you feel like giggling a little, that is fine. Now, say it like you mean it. Feels good, doesn't it?

But I am getting ahead of myself. I need to share with you more of my story, how I discovered my super power, and how my world was saved from utter destruction!

I am not a fiction writer. I can't make this stuff up.

Chapter 2

Twisted Special Gifts

"I always thought it was my fault. Was I not being clear?
Did I do something to encourage this? In many ways I respected
him. There were times that I felt he was a protector, other times
a best friend I could laugh with. I just couldn't understand
why he wouldn't respect me when we were alone."
-Annie #metoo

MY CHILDHOOD PHOTO ALBUM SHOWS a family outing to Bridal Veil Falls. I am three years old, dressed in patchwork trousers that were all the rage in 1976 for little girls. Several pictures were taken that day. In each of them I hold my pink doll in a haphazard but motherly way.

In one picture, a charming scene is perfectly framed. I am on my tippy toes, craning my view over a railing to see the river below, my doll over my shoulder as though I might burp her at any moment. A man stands behind

me, his body mirroring mine, his hand protectively on my shoulder, inches from both my doll's false locks and my unruly ones. He looks like an attentive uncle, watching over me. That is what everyone saw. He was very attentive, thoughtful even. He foresaw needs my family had, gained sympathy from my parents, and was adopted in as an honored uncle. He gave us all gifts, but he gave me special gifts.

He had a fancy red sports car that talked with a keypad to unlock it. This was cool, fascinating stuff in those days. He gave me the combo to the keypad because he trusted me. No one else had those numbers, only me because I was special.

As an adult, I have thought back through the abuse and realized the worst thing he did was the mental manipulation. He plied my brain to protect him, he manipulated my thinking, and then he brought me into his twisted truths until I believed I was the guilty one.

I don't believe in public group therapy, where someone has gone through a traumatic event and tells everyone the entire gruesome thing. Private group therapy and individual therapy are both helpful tools, but simply spreading your story to any innocent bystander isn't an effective means of healing. I see it happen all the time on the stage. Sometimes it happens in books. I didn't want to put in my own story, but God won't leave me alone. He gets so pushy sometimes. I've decided to include it only for the lessons that it teaches. And I'm allowing myself to eat all the chocolate that I want.

Becoming a Victim

I am not sure of the age I was at when MTDMI started to touch my body. I know it was young. I know it was before I went to Miss Janet's preschool class. I have this vague memory of my preschool teacher explaining that our bodies were our own. Stronger is the memory of him navigating this lesson that was meant to protect me and other little kids in the class. He reframed it to fit his motives and actions. I accepted his definition. After all, he was an adult, and my parents trusted him with me. I didn't fully understand what trust was, nor the concept of who was trustworthy. I saw that he said one thing to my parents and another to me, but I didn't understand it as a sign of not being trustworthy. I was a little girl. As a survivor, it is important to look at what we know now in contrast to what we understood then. We can't blame ourselves for what we didn't understand.

My father owned a mobile home trucking company, so at a young age I was expected to help with the chores. MTDMI would often give me massages to help my tiny body feel better from the day's labor. As an adult, I can understand this is what is called grooming.

So much of who I am today is a result of what happened to me in those fundamental childhood years and also who was in my life. MTDMI was part of my childhood, part of family vacations, fun times, sacred times, and then at night he snuck into my room. Should I now throw out every year, every vacation, every moment that he was part of? It's a very complex editing job, not simply Photoshopping his image out of a photograph. That cuts out more than just him, it cuts out a piece of me.

I grew up in an ideal neighborhood with loving parents. We were poor, but the community around us was always kind. MTDMI fit in so easily because he often anticipated the needs of my parents, and he exploited the weaknesses and dysfunctions that ran through my childhood. Dysfunctions? Allow me to elaborate.

My grandparents have a ranking system of how they distribute love. I've never quite cracked the code, but I know the system is compiled based on birth order, job status, genetics, and, above all, looks. It is all so dysfunctional but as I was growing up each of us in the family played our part to keep the system going.

It took my grandparents years to ever pay my father a compliment. They saw him as a grunt laborer, not seeing how good he was at his job. Men who worked desk jobs were held at a higher opinion. MTDMI happened to work at a desk job. He knew this dynamic of blue collar vs. white collar and let me know he would take care of me. Because my grandparents and MTDMI undercut my perception of my father's ability to provide a living, I naturally followed the train of thought that I had to keep MTDMI happy. I had to be sweet. He played up my fears for security, food, and shelter. I began hiding food in my room. Still to this day I like a full pantry.

The man I knew as my grandfather was my grandmother's second husband, not my genetic grandfather. It's not that it matters; however, it mattered to my grandparents. Being a parent is not about common blood, it is about service and love.

My mom always said this man was a good father to her. She wasn't allowed to see her genetic father, who had the neighboring farm. One day when she was in her small town's grocery store, she walked around the corner and saw him. She was frozen in such fear that she urinated herself. She'd been told that her father had killed people. What her mother chose to leave out was that he had killed people in war and was a decorated glider pilot.

I think my mom has an inflated need to see the good in others, taught to her from necessity by her home life. She chose to be kind, which speaks greatly to her credit. She truly sees the best in others. She was a teacher of teens with behavior disorders and this gift helped her professionally.

I mention genetics because, although it doesn't really matter, looks and genetics mattered a lot to my grandparents. Like my mother, I took after the wrong side. My brother Lance also takes after the wrong side. I guess we look more like our biological grandfather, the father my mother never knew until she was an adult. As a result, we were projects that would not amount to the same as my cousins and other siblings. My other two brothers were compared to my dad's side with their sturdy shoulders, which would be good for hard labor. Only my sister was college material, and they paid for her college education as well as for several of my cousins. I desperately sought my grandparents' approval, as their approval came with gifts. I was trained to think that financial gifts meant love, again something that MTDMI manipulated. To this day, I hate gifts that come with an apology or a string attached. The gifts I seek in friendship are honesty, character, and unconditional love.

Attention from my grandparents came in the form of commentary on my unpleasant personality, food intake, and weight. I was muscular for a child but not fat. One day my cousins and I were to go play in my grandparents' pool. I was there first and my grandfather began flinging me up in the air, his hands catching me as he flung me out of the water time and time again. I was ecstatic. Then my cousins arrived, just as he was preparing to fling me in the air. His hands instantly dropped, and he said, "You're so heavy." His full attention was then given to my cousins.

At lunch came more comments about my eating. As we all left that day, my grandfather hugged my cousins close, but as was his way with me, he held me at my shoulders. I felt he found me repulsive.

MTDMI was in town, so after the upsetting afternoon he took me out for ice cream. He only commented on my beauty and didn't stare at my eating. I felt grown up, special, older than my cousins. Perhaps all of this was just what a woman feels? They say that love hurts, so the pit in my stomach from MTDMI's secret touches meant nothing. I became skilled at discounting my own internal voice.

I had developed curves sooner than my peers, and Grandma frequently commented on my chest. Grandma lectured me on how indecent my breasts were, the pitfalls of such a shape, and how wary I would need to be. These two lumps had brought me nothing good. I didn't have a whole lot of options on clothing, as finances were limited, so I started to wear the baggiest clothes I could, which were usually hand-me-downs from my brothers.

When I was nine, I was involved in a bicycle accident that knocked out three of my front teeth, leaving a wide gap in my smile. I also neglected my grooming. I was that greasy-haired kid in the halls of my school. I was labeled "unfortunate" in my demeanor, looks, and personality so much that I fully identified it as true.

I began trying to prove to my two older brothers that I was as tough as any boy. I stopped with anything pink and glittery, and tried to walk tough. Both my grandmother and MTDMI would comment on my walk. He would even take my hips in his hands and try to make me walk right. I acted dumb like I just couldn't do it. Perhaps those moments were the first stages of my push back.

Our home was in a beautiful neighborhood. In front of our house was a little dip. That's what we called it, the dip. In winter, cars would drive and slide in front of our houses. We didn't park our cars in the "slide zone" in winter because it was bound to get hit. My brothers were tough, strong men. We all were tough, conditioned from the family business of mobile home moving and set up. We would time the boys running out to get the vehicles out of the dip and send them on their way, laughing as the cars slid away. We enjoyed stories of my brothers recounting the cheers and the tips that the grateful drivers would give them.

Our home had windows from floor to ceiling, and as I'd watch the snowy sliding adventures, MTDMI would be there telling me to be safe, telling me I couldn't go outside because I was too precious to be hurt. I was a girl and was so special to him. I can hear his words, feel his touch telling me how unique I was. I received extra time, attention, and treats from MTDMI and it made my brothers jealous. He would take me on drives to be secluded. It is sickening to think of now. What would happen in that so-called "special time" turns my stomach.

I felt that just like our home was floor to ceiling windows, so was my soul, so was my pain. Why could no one see? I felt stuck in a dip. Frozen. And no one was coming to push me out.

I have other memories of MTDMI's grooming. Once I was in a bookstore with MTDMI, and he purchased a book for me. The title? *The Miracle of Forgiveness.*

"You need to read this book, Leta," said MTDMI, "because you need to understand what you do wrong." I was probably about twelve at that time. There were other words said, but it reinforced that I was the one to blame. He often told me that he couldn't help himself, and that he did the things he did to me because of what I did to him.

He twisted my concepts of religion and forgiveness to believe that I had blame. He used religion to manipulate me. For those of us that are religious, this is another reason why we need to be clear about sins and wrongdoing and how the power of the Atonement of Jesus Christ is there to envelope all the hard that happens to us. We need to teach that we are only responsible for our own actions.

MTDMI said that I was so beautiful, and men are only sexual beings that can't help but respond to my beauty. In contrast, my grandmother often told me how ugly I was, that I was so ugly I was unlovable, and I would never be able to find a husband. Ironically, it was the verbal onslaught of my grandmother that saved me. I was raised to believe that adults are right. And here were two adults telling me opposite things. It was the divergence of these two thoughts that made me realize that maybe one, or both, of them was wrong. That maybe, just maybe, it was somewhere in the middle.

Chapter 3

Creating the Circles of Intimacy

"I can't describe the shock as we first looked at our own [picture], then one by one at each of the others. We'd all drawn ourselves without a face."
–Sandi Stillings #metoo

YEARS AGO, I CAME UP with this bull's-eye model to help others realize when someone had crossed a line. As I have said, the physical violations of my molestations were not as damaging as my physiological and emotional violations and this model helps us understand where those lines should be.

Tool #1: Creating the Circles of Intimacy using love, trust, and accountibility

Imagine a dartboard bull's-eye, with all its rings getting bigger as they go out. You stand in your innermost circle. In each of these rings are the people of your life, and as we move toward the center are those closest to you. We do some of this placement naturally; people we don't

know have less influence. We don't equally take to heart the thoughts and opinions of others. The opinions of those most intimate to us hold the greatest weight. Intimacy is often thought of as sexual, but in this book, I want to be clear that intimacy means friendship, familiarity, togetherness, affection, understanding, and attachment.

You stand in your innermost circle. We are born with a circle around us; we automatically place our parents and siblings in a close circle to us. Sadly, that may not always mean that these people are safe. As we age, we become increasingly able to distinguish who should be close to us or not. We may have an affinity for this cousin over that cousin. We may even find it necessary to remove people from our lives or move them further out from our bull's-eye.

As mentioned, you stand in your innermost circle. Who is allowed to be there with you? Do you include your mom, dad, uncles, sisters, aunts, or your neighbor? Who can be in that innermost circle of trust, love, and accountability with you? The people in the center are who you think of first when choosing how to act. An abuser moves themselves up the rings to be close to you, close to your thoughts, and your boundaries slip.

So who gets to be in that inner circle, the center of the bull's-eye with you? It's a trick question. The answer is that only someone who can love perfectly, be 100% accountable, and is always trustworthy for your care, benefit, and safety. No human can do that. When someone is in that innermost circle, that person is in your mind. Those reading this that have been abused, you know what I am saying: every thought is filtered through the lens of what the abuser will think. Every action. Every motive checked. We fear consequences if we don't do as he dictates. So who can be in that circle with you?

I believe God is capable of being in your innermost circle, but only God. No one else gets to live in your head. I do filter a lot of my life through how God would want me to act, how God would want me to think, how God would want me to respond. God has the track record of love, trust, and accountability. I am aware that some of you reading this are angry with God. You may not like Him very much, you may feel that He really screwed up and that He really let you down. I get that because I have felt that way. In fact, I have told Him off several times, and with strong language, hateful feelings and not in a respectful tone. God can take it.

For understanding this module, if you need to, you can remove God from your inner visual circle. That is okay. The point is *no human* gets to be in that innermost circle with you. Not your beloved mom, or your abusive mom, not your amazing dad, or your dad that molested you, not your adoring spouse, or your controlling spouse; no one good or bad is in that circle with you. You, and you alone in a good state of mind, should think through how others' words, actions, and feelings impact you.

Let's not confuse this with selfishness. If you say something mean or unkind, that still impacts you as well, because we all impact each other in this world. We cannot hurt another person to any level of our intimacy circle and not have it impact us in a negative way through either guilt, lack of character, or just through the ripple effect of what most call Karma. Life is hardest on those that have to live in a brain full of hate. It is also not about doing whatever feels good; everyone has feelings that often betray our best intentions, motives, and what we really want from life.

The innermost bull's-eye is a gauge to see if you are choosing to be in control of you, or if you are abdicating ruling your own brain, choices, and happiness to someone else. When you are being abused, you give that God-given right to your own thoughts over to someone who is not strong enough to hold that power of you with justice and consistency. This is because we humans fail, we screw up, and we make mistakes. And some of us choose to be selfish to the point of hurting others. Abusing another in any way is selfishness.

How can you know where to place people in your circle of intimacy? Ask yourself three questions, then judge others based on their actions. You have to observe people to see if they perform well in these three areas. You can't ask them, as action and intentions are often very different.

1) Do they love you consistently?

Abusers manipulate your love to their own means, including your love for them, your love for God, your love for others. Love is not selfish, love is kind, love is patient. What does love really mean? If you're in the middle of being abused, you may not know what real love is. You'll need to do some soul searching on this topic. I can promise you love is the most awesome feeling on this planet: it's amazing and it doesn't ever come with shame. Shame is a tool of manipulation. Can a manipulator love you? He may say love, but it is a selfish emotion. He will work to possess you, control you, so he can own you. Think about what we call unconditional love. It loves without expectation. It loves without quid pro quo. It is love without strings attached.

We all expect something from each other, but evil twists that into a misunderstanding of what love is. Is love sexual attraction? Imagine someone telling you "I love you, we need to have sex." Any variation of this, and I hope you hear me, is not love. Real, pure love is acting for the benefit of the other person.

I show my family I love them when I cook dinner. I don't really like cooking that much. Cooking and then demanding my family thank me is not showing love, since I was expecting that they do something for me in return. It is nice if they thank me, because that's a way they can show me love and respect. A mother cares for her child, and if she gets a thank you, at the very least she is going to have to wait for that kid to be able to talk. As any not-marred-by-crazy mom can tell you, no thanks is needed. The feelings of love have grown beyond expression: that child doesn't have to do anything for that love. With my own kids, I can say that I will always love them no matter what they do or become. Am I perfect? Heavens no, but I am trying every single day. The only thing us humans can do is try to show our love in meaningful ways. When you do mess up, what do you do? That leads us to the next question.

2) Are they Accountable?

This is perhaps the most revealing character trait. Love is so hard to define, but accountability is pretty easy. Does she take responsibility for her words and actions? Or does she say, "It's your fault," "You made me," "I can't help myself," "Well you did…"? If she is never at fault, she is always innocent, then that's a huge red flag. In fact, I am so big on this that if people can't own up to their actions, I have no interest in having them my life. Harsh, I know. Perhaps I have a history with this?

Even God can say He is sorry. He even apologizes that we didn't understand, in Jeremiah 42:10 He says, "for I repent me of the evil that I have done unto you." Seriously, that's an example for which to strive. Everyone who has abused, manipulated, or molested me cannot take responsibility. I recommend that you listen in conversations for such convincing lies, as manipulators are so good at weaving stories and feelings that even they believe them. We can make ourselves believe anything. The following is a silly example, but perfect to drive home the point.

I had a very enigmatic coworker that did something against company policy. It wasn't a big deal, so I simply called her out on it. She spent weeks trying to convince me I didn't actually see her break the rule, then switched to say it would be easier for everyone if that wasn't a rule at all, making small alterations to her story. But the company wouldn't change. It led to her not wanting to work with me, spreading drama and lies to a ridiculous amount over something that wasn't even my rule. Yet, she couldn't just say, "Oh I did it wrong, and I shouldn't have." It wouldn't have been a big deal, but instead she tried to convince everyone that she was the victim. It all was very painful drama.

For my part, I realized I was guilty of overlooking her lack of accountability for years because I liked her so much. Yet all the warnings had been there early on. She was the victim and the hero of every story. She was always right, but she told the story in such an emotional way and I overlooked this warning sign. She turned on me because I may have been one of the few people in her life to say a powerful word: No. People that are averse to accountability don't accept no. They are the exception, they will twist the story, events, facts, and situation so that they always come out clean. Any person she had a falling out with was crazy. All of them, lots of crazy people.

MTDMI has never apologized. I doubt he ever will, because in his mind it was love. In truth it was selfishness, lust, and his inability to see what damage it caused my young self and it shows his twisted nature. His inability to empathize with my pain shows a mix of sociopathic evil and absolutely no accountability.

Watch others to see how they can be accountable for their impact on others. That is what I tell young people to look for when dating others. The ability to say, "I am sorry" will mean more than the sonnets of excuses. "I am sorry," when it is sincere and stands alone. It is heartfelt and real. I had my list of traits of warning when someone was avoiding accountability and then my sister-in-law, Katie Greene, shared a talk with me by Lynn G. Robbins and it blew my list out of the water. It was so complete. His talk, "Be 100% Responsible[1]" is now a favorite. Google it.

He calls it the "anti-responsibility list," and it is as follows.

Blame	Cover up
Complain/ Murmur	Self-Pity/ Victim
Rationalization	Flee/ Avoid
Find Fault/ Get Angry	Indecision
Make Excuses	Abandon
Make Demands	Procrastinate
Minimize/ trivialize	Deny/ Lie
Entitlements	Fear
Hide	Rebel
Doubt, lose hope, quit	Enable

We may exhibit some of these traits, but when we give into that trait, we are giving up our choices, our power, our happiness and we are not being accountable for the outcome of our lives. Both victims and abusers fall into this. But it is not about blame, it is about taking responsibility for where we are now and what will be done about it. The abuser doesn't take responsibility without conditions. The victim may blame themselves, or an abuser, and lull themselves into not putting the pieces of their shattered life back together. This will only bring misery until we stop giving into these traits. In spiritual terms, it is called repentance. We must change or turn from our misdeeds, sins or habits that don't serve us.

After her kidnapping, Elizabeth Smart's mother said to her:

> *Elizabeth, what this man has done is terrible. There aren't any words that are strong enough to describe how wicked and evil he is! He has taken nine months of your life that*

---

1 Lynn G. Robbins, "Be 100% Responsible" filmed at BYU August 2017 https:// speeches.byu.edu/talks/lynn-g-robbins_be-100-percent-responsible/

*you will never get back again. But the best punishment
you could ever give him is to be happy. To move forward
with your life. To do exactly what you want. Because, yes,
this will probably go to trial and some kind of sentencing
will be given to him and that wicked woman. But even if
that's true, you may never feel like justice has been served
or that true restitution has been made...*

    *You be happy, Elizabeth. Just be happy. If you go and
feel sorry for yourself, or if you dwell on what has happened, if you hold on to your pain, that is allowing him
to steal more of your life away. So don't you do that! Don't
you let him! There is no way that he deserves that. Not
one more second of your life. You keep every second for
yourself. You keep them and be happy."*

                                      —*Elizabeth Smart*[2]

3) Are they trustworthy?

    This is part of accountability, but think about what could be in the
way of someone being reliable? Usually it's an addiction. He may love
you, he may even know his addiction is wrong, but he has given his will
over to the addiction. Sex, porn, drugs, alcohol, abuse, power, cutting,
hoarding, eating disorders, gambling, drama, attention, people pleas-
ing, smoking, and in my case, chocolate, all are addictive.[3] If someone
is under the influence of the addiction, he is not making choices with
his conscious brain. He is choosing almost out of instinct, as would an
animal. As much as he loves you, as much as he wants to love, protect,
honor, and cherish you, he cannot. He has chosen the addiction.

    In my first book, *"How to Embrace Your Inner Hotness,"* I talk about
the 3/5-years rule I applied during dating. Five years before meeting
you is really none of my business. We all can grow and become better,

---

2   Elizabeth Smart, *My Story* (St Martin's Press, 2013) 285–286

3   See http://addictionz.com/types-of-addictions/

but for the last three years, what have been your habits? What are you working on and in what direction are you headed? If this person is what you want for the future role model of your children, then by all means keep dating. If they are still entangled in habits and addictions you are not okay with, you are bringing those habits and addictions into your life regardless of the other person's promises to the contrary. He chose what he was when it was just him, and with all the people around him, he chose that life. Even if he loves you, if he wouldn't change for everyone else, why, why would he change for you? Sometimes it is defined as romantic to save a guy from himself and his troubled life. This is the kind of romance that yields reality show participants (think Dr. Phil). So, ask yourself, does she have the character you admire? Is there anything in the way of her being trustworthy? What do her past actions say? This goes two ways. If you are working on your own character, you should get a partner who has been working on theirs.

When you are placing people in your circles of intimacy, you alone decide where others go. This is not a discussion you have with others, "Hey just so you know, you are in the third ring out from me. You were in the first ring, but I bumped you for inconsistencies in the accountability section." Nor do you say, "If you do this, you get bumped up into a closer circle." That would be manipulative on your part. If they're aware of this theory or not they will say things like:

"I thought you loved me."

"Don't you trust me?"

"But I love you"

"I thought I was your best friend."

"You just have to accept me for who I am."

These are those trying to violate your boundaries: you decide where they go and those that can do all three (love, trust, and accountability) with consistency, may be in the ring closest to you. I hope for each of you young people that your parents are such people. I was coaching a teenage girl, and her mother was the one who brought her. I knew very little about her life. I am not a therapist and was not trying to dig into her life. I give principles of truth, that's how I coach. One day as I was showing her the Circles of Intimacy, she said, "Oh, so my dad with his porn addiction…" she understood it. We then talked about how he was close to her in both the love and the accountability sections, but his lack of trustworthiness due to his addiction helped her to see how she needed to lower her expectations of him, to moderate risk of harm, and love him in a safe way. She understood it wasn't about her, it was an addiction, and as long as she expected him to choose her over his addiction to porn, she would be continually hurt and let down.

It can be difficult to always remember and maintain your circles and boundaries. Allowing someone you just met to take precedence over everyone else is a sign of, well, being a teenager. Romeo and Juliet are a famous example of love at first sight, not listening to their parents, and, at the end, are dead. All joking aside, it is a sign of being sexualized, because having given of your body, you become blind to the traits of the other person and fall deeply in "love." Love without knowing someone's character is playing Russian roulette with your heart. It takes time to assess another person's character. No matter how much time you have invested, you should distance yourself when you recognize you're in an abusive situation. That is easily said, but most people love those that abuse them: the proximity is what gives them that chance. Applying learning tools and doing self-work on your mental well-being is essential to distance yourself and to see the abuse clearly.

Shame is defined as "a painful emotion caused by the consciousness of guilt, shortcoming, or impropriety."[4] Shame can be especially damaging when wrongly inflicted on us by another, like when blame, criticism, or manipulation purposefully diverges from reality. Shame is an unpleasant emotion. It isn't always clear where it comes from; it

---

4   Meriam-Webster Dictionary, s.v. "Shame," accessed July 2018, https://www.merriam-webster.com/dictionary/shame

breaks into our quiet moments and shuts us down. When deep hurt happens to us, shame enters, often coming with guilt and despair.

Shame makes us feel that we are trapped in a whirlpool. It pulls at us, we feel defeated, lost, and even hopeless. The danger of shame is that it turns us into something else, into what we hate. We are filled with self-loathing, a common side effect of abuse. We must find someone who loves us and is safe, like a parent, a school therapist, a psychologist, or clergy.

To fight shame, you can again apply the same steps as the Circles of Intimacy.

> *1) LOVE: We need to talk about it in a safe place or with someone who loves us. Parent, teacher, therapist, friend, clergy.*

> *2) ACCOUNTABILITY: We must work through where responsibility lies and where it doesn't.*

> *3) TRUST: Work to rewire our brain to understand that we were caught in an addiction, and that we alone have the power to move ourselves forward from shame to hope.*

As we balance our own rings of intimacy, in our own thoughts, actions, and words, we will like us more. As you work through the above process to strengthen yourself mentally, emotionally, and psychologically, you move yourself away from the darkness that shame creates.

Chapter 4

When Goblins Become Real

"My uncle slipped me drugs at eleven years old. That was
the start of six torturous years of molestation. I've told everybody
for thirty years about this, nobody has ever believed me.
He molested my friend, too."
–Pauline Bowman #metoo

I WAS EIGHT WHEN MTDMI's molesting turned from touches to more adult acts. He had decided that I was to be his wife, and at some level I understood that and felt trapped. The bitter consequence of sexual abuse is that it pushes a victim off a cliff in physical, sexual, and psychological ramifications. Self-loathing colored my world as I navigated the school halls following the lines of the yellow, blue, and orange brick. I accepted the shoulder bumps down those halls as routine.

By eleven I was what would now be described as suicidal. I wanted to cease, to die, but I couldn't figure out how to do so without making a mess. I didn't even feel worthy of making a mess. The MTDMI was grooming me not only to keep his secret, but also to be his wife. He was particular of how I loaded dishes into the dishwasher he'd bought my family, a neat luxury back then. He instructed me on how to make beds and how to clean toilets. It was isolating and horrifying, but it wasn't the only thing making life hard at that point.

I have two older brothers, and the one just older than me was heavily involved in drugs. He had me transport them, because no one would suspect a little kid had drugs in her backpack. And don't forget that I was pretty weird. I didn't have all of my front teeth, I had a few facial scars, and I often wore my brothers' hand-me-down clothes. Throw in the greasy hair and no wonder my peers avoided me. My real grandmother didn't like me and set the tone as to how the rest of the family should treat me. To put it lightly, I was odd and felt completely alone. In retrospect, considering everything that was going on in my life, I'm pretty impressed at how well I was holding it together!

At heart, my brother was a tender tough guy, a teddy bear that was growing into the physique that the men in my family are known for and hugs that you can feel to your spine. No one could mess with me too much without going through my charming and gregarious older brother.

In a story that is not mine to tell, this teddy bear became solemn, withdrawn, and angry due to drugs. He was so charming that initially he was able to hide his addiction from my parents. For me it was another secret to keep, another person who confided dark things to me that I was to keep inside. I fell into protecting his secret with the skill taught to me by MTDMI.

When we give into evil, relinquish who we want to be, our thoughts become twisted. No soul comes to this earth evil. Human yes, but not evil. Even MTDMI. Once he was a child. I don't know when he first chose to give into pedophilic temptation or where that path started. That isn't a conversation I will ever have, or want to have, with him. That is a conversation between him and God.

In the case of my brother, whom I will always love and see the tender boy he was, he never intended for the events that happened one fall night in my fifth-grade year. He and some friends were using a substance, I don't know what it was. I was nearby. It may have been their words, maybe a feeling, maybe both. I knew that I needed to leave, and fast.

As I turned away, his friends came after me. I ran up a hill that I'd run up a hundred times in pursuit of childhood games, sometimes the robber, sometimes the cop. This time I knew with clarity what was at stake. I knew that, unlike the sickly soft touches of MTDMI with quiet whispers, this would be harsh and painful. This would be more than one.

I was running for a small grove of trees that I knew well. In my mind I would be safe there. Why didn't I head for a neighbor's house? A thought I have with clarity only in hindsight. As the leaves crumpled under my feet, the boys had circled around, coordinating their approach, trapping me in the center of the once magical trees. I crouched just off the main trail knowing I was exposed, but what could I do?

I held my limbs into my torso, willing myself to disappear, knowing that my breath would betray my location. Without a clear reason I kept saying, "God. God. God." It wasn't a formal prayer. It was a desperate pleading. My would-be rapist walked so close to me, then turned and yelled to the other boy not far behind, "Do you see her?"

He hadn't seen me? He hadn't seen me! He hadn't heard my ragged breaths! I remained there in my little safe spot until the lights on my mom's pickup illuminated our driveway. The scene she came home to was distressing enough to find paraphernalia just outside her front door. I put on a smile as though I had been playing with fairies in the woods.

Being an adept secret keeper, I didn't tell anyone what happened until I was an adult. I am sharing this with you because of the conclusions I made that night. That night is burned into my soul, as horrid as what could have been pales in the realization that I had kind of prayed and I had been protected. There was an angel that had leaned over me, blocking me from that drugged boy's sight or a divine hand that covered his ears, so he passed by, deaf to my mutterings. I had been unexplainably saved.

How did I know to call out to God?

A memory of my family surfaces first, the smell of a fresh log crackling as the fire licked it to embers, the cold pushed outside of that room. My dad's gentle voice reads from the scriptures. It was a book with words that meant little to me then, but I loved those early mornings for the tone, the feel. I still savor the feeling of that time as the beginnings of my understanding of God.

Another building block of my understanding of God comes from a church teacher. In my church, the other congregants are called Brother or Sister. Sister Sorenson undoubtedly spent hours writing out little thoughts and scriptures for her primary class. I am sad only one sample of her beautiful handwriting can be found in my childhood papers. With bent edges of over forty years, the paper says, "I am a child of God. I have unique talents." A snowflake we made in class is glued in the center. She passionately worked with us young kids, helping us commit to memory phrases like, "We believe in God the Eternal Father and in His Son Jesus Christ."

While I've highlighted many of the negative influences around those foundational years, there were many good people in my life. My childhood was filled with our church family. Sister Lee with her purple lipstick that still makes me smile, I loved it so much. Brother Lee was something of a local celebrity for his career in Washington D.C. and later as President of our local university. He taught me to study and analyze the scriptures, to ask hard questions, and to always ask questions. Sister Debry hired me as her mommy's helper. I decorate just like her and hunt thrift stores with an eye trained by her. I tie grocery bags and see her hands doing the same. I pull weeds and hear us laughing. She would just keep working even though she was paying me to work. I worked for her until I left home. She was like a mother and to this day I have to tell her of the happenings of my life.

Sister Dalzen taught me how to handle a knife and cheered the loudest when I won the log sawing competition, which is my first memory of being the best at anything. It was she who placed the log piece in my hand as a trophy. Sister Hansen sang with the most beautiful look on her face. Sister Clayton had treats to share whenever you went to her house. Once when my dad was sick, she took me to her filled-to-the-brim pantry and told me to point to everything that our family would eat. As I wasn't bold enough, she started asking would they eat this, yes of course they would. She placed my timid selections and her abundant ones side by side in a box for me to take home. It was her husband, our family doctor, who cried when he diagnosed me with an autoimmune disease while holding my hands and calling me princess. He always called me princess, even though I was a flannel and old t-shirt wearing kind of girl.

Sister Chambers' laughter with her son, who was just my age, was pure joy. When another boy our age, who was very dear to me, died tragically in a car accident, it was her son Davy who told me things would be okay and gave me a hug in the purity of an eight-year-old. There was a different Brother Lee who came to our home each month to share a gospel message that involved us kids.

And Grandma Winnie, who although wasn't my genetic grandmother, was adopted into the family as she became legally blind. She made cinnamon rolls that all of us kids still yearn for. It was at her death when I was eight that I can distinctly recognize that God comforted me. It was also her death that emboldened MTDMI to begin visiting me in the night.

MTDMI took these amazing people's love and turned it into guilt in my heart. He took their lessons and reinterpreted the principles in my mind. This was his greatest violation, warping the limited love, goodness, and light of my life into a mystery. I had been given the foundation of a good life, yet it was almost all but faded from my day-to-day thoughts.

As things in my life were getting worse, I did not have the skills to categorize what was happening to me. I was a little girl. It was so much easier to say these things weren't real. I decided the real things were fake, and I created a world that I wanted to be in when I was around nine years old. Over the years I would go to this little imaginary place when bad things were happening. I would run through the forest on the back of a unicorn as Princess Leta.

At first it was an escape. Adults should know coping skills to escape their demons: we can talk about it, create boundaries, and remove ourselves from toxic people. These same coping skills aren't available to children who are told to keep secrets. So what do we do? We bury these emotions. Then they come out as anger, resentment, and/or depression.

Today I can still see this beautiful little fantasyland. Now it's a memory, but back then it was very real and tangible. But because I didn't have the skills to talk about it, or to protect myself, elements of my fantasy world came into my everyday life. And elements of my everyday life came into my fantasy world. Suddenly, even in the imaginary place my demons caught up to me. Then the lines of my imagination and reality became blurred, and it became difficult for me to distinguish what was real.

I have faithfully kept a censored journal since I was a little girl. As I was writing this book, I pulled one out from that time period. In it is a drawing of a mean little goblin that would fly around. Sometimes he would show up in my classroom. Whenever I thought about telling on my brother, or on MTDMI, Goblin Guy would show up.

There were also these little gold bugs that would follow me. While I was asleep I would pick at myself, then when I woke up, I had scratches and was bleeding. To me, it was proof that the bugs had attacked. They'd follow me around and after school I'd run home, terrified.

Only now as an adult do I understand. There was a man in the neighborhood, and he had a gold Volkswagen bug in which he would follow me home from school. It was so much easier to imagine these little bugs than to understand there was one more person in the world that wanted to molest me. As history played out, that was exactly his intention. He molested some girls in my neighborhood.

It was easier to imagine I was being chased by a horde of bugs than by another abuser.

Now in sixth grade, I could see the peers around me moving away from imagination and child-ish things. Not only could I not give them up, I was trapped. If I thought about telling, the Goblin Guy's spy would come, or the Gob-lin Guy would visit me in really dramatic scenes. In one of these dramatic scenes, I remember I was  in my stone castle, and the people of my kingdom had united to fight the Goblin Guy. And he's burning them. I could hear the screams. The servants in the castle were my friends because I didn't have many real-life friends. I could hear them dying in this battle scene. The Goblin Guy got in my castle, trapped me in a corner, and I knew this was my doom. He was coming for me.

Fortunately, I turned to the one coping skill I did have and prayed to God. I knew that God was real because I had run into a forest and prayed, and my brother's friends didn't find me.

This time when I was trapped in my castle, and called out to God, another miracle happened. The Goblin Guy started shrinking. He was screaming, writhing in anger, the eyes glaring at me. I was frozen, terri-fied. My kingdom had been destroyed, but the Goblin Guy continued shrinking down. Then the castle cat came, killed the Goblin Guy, and then ate him.

It was like I was in this faraway place, but at that moment, I understood that what I had known and experienced was not real. It was upsetting to realize that the people I had loved and cared about, and had died in a very gruesome way, were not real.

I never went back to my fantasy world after that.

The self-hatred poured into the pages of my sixth-grade journal speaks to how broken down I was emotionally, physically, and mentally. With God as my only coping skill, this was a turning point of when I began to take ownership for myself. I started dealing with things as they really were. I didn't handle things smoothly—I was a kid—but it started me on a path of recognizing God.

I took a psychology class in college, and I remember them describing a mental breakdown. I remember feeling like a giant chasm had opened in my mind. Because I finally acknowledged that I'd had a mental breakdown, I now felt broken. Maybe the chasm had always been there, but I was just now realizing it. As the professor talked of the ramifications, I took more than careful notes, wanting to understand. It's not a pleasant thing to understand, but being stripped down to nothing gave me a kind of humility and odd hope. If I could be undone, then couldn't I be remade? I began a path of taking care of my well-being and my mental health. It made me realize that I have to be responsible for what is happening in my own head. I had let so many other people in there. The inner workings of our mind are not meant to be a crowded place.

I haven't thought about my breakdown in a long time, because I've developed habits and skills that have transformed me into the powerhouse that I am today. I was afraid to share this story because I didn't want people to say, "See, a crazy person wrote this book. Why should we listen to her?" Yes, the spy of the Goblin Guy would follow me around. He got into my real world and forced me to extremes, but that is where I found God.

It is in intense pain that we find out some things about ourselves that are worth knowing. Maybe you will hear this story and think that a crazy person wrote a book. I'm hoping that, instead, you'll see that even someone as broken as I was could find a solid foundation on which to rebuild her life: God.

I was literally failing in every aspect of life. I was failing elementary school, which is hard to do. Psychologically, I was breaking. I knew I was dumb, I knew I was an idiot, I knew I was a reject, and that I didn't fit in anywhere. I felt like the only person who accepted me was the one who was actually taking the most from me. He showed me "love," which I now understand is a complete adulteration of that word. But that was my perception—that love hurt and cost you.

Eventually, I got to a point where I could talk about my brother's drug addiction. He started getting in trouble with the law, and so it felt okay to add in my little pieces of what I knew. But I had been waiting for life to give me permission to tell someone that my boundaries had been violated. It didn't work for me mentally, physically, or spiritually. But even in the darkness of all that, a basis of my understanding of God comes from hiding in trees as a boy walked past me and feeling protected, and while in my imaginary castle, seeing my Goblin Guy shrink down because I called out to my God.

I can't change what happened to that little girl, to little Leta who didn't understand the borders between fantasy and reality. But I can change her world now. I can change what happens to her. I can look at her with compassion instead of saying, "You're a crazy person who had a mental breakdown in sixth grade, you're worthless."

Chapter 5

Raising my Voice

*I didn't clock out and never went back to collect my last
paycheck. It wasn't worth it. I quit my job because of
unwanted sexual advances by a woman.*
—Josephine Ackman Franco #metoo

THE NEXT-DOOR KIDS WERE MY closest playmates other than my
little brother. We would run from yard to yard depending on our
games. We had endless hours of imagination. Where our two yards met
was a city sewage drain. We loved to drop rocks in there and hear them
chime back as they hit the bottom. It was fascinating. Since we lived in
a dip, if any neighbor was running their sprinklers, we could splash in
the water on its way to the drain.

One hot day when I was thirteen, we were in our swimsuits
crouched over the drain. Perhaps we had been throwing rocks down
or watching sticks find their way to the bottomless hole. MTDMI had
come to town. At this point his arrival would instigate both trepida-
tion and excitement. Being so brainwashed, I may have thought it was
love. But it was a secret love, just like the starlets in movies. I knew
several secret love stories. At this point, I thought of him as mine. He

had found the holes in my heart and had taught me how they were to be filled. He had taught me he was the answer.

Standing there in our swimsuits, MTDMI came over to talk to us girls. He proposed to take us to the local water park, so we could have some real fun! All of us thought that was a great idea. I can remember the angles, the body positions, and where we were each standing as he placed his hand on one of the neighbor girl's shoulder. I saw the side of his face looking at her.

I knew. I knew what that look meant. That awareness pierced through any delusion I may have had. I knew what he was planning.

I revered these kids and I adored their mom. She was quick to pass out treats, compliments, and laughter. I thought that I was "lucky" to have anyone notice me. I knew that I was ugly to everyone else but beautiful to MTDMI, and here he was looking at another girl. Yes, it was jealousy that turned my stomach, but it was also a protective feeling. She was of worth. I wasn't, but she was.

It was then that I knew what had been happening was wrong. I have tried to sort out how I knew, as it was all so twisted in my mind. I don't have an answer, but in that moment, it was clear. I felt revulsion for myself, for him, and his hand on her shoulder. In my mind, it was up to me to protect her. I grabbed his hand in mine. I often held his hand as nieces do with their uncles. Nobody had ever questioned it. He looked so pleased this time when I took his hand. His eyes had a look in them. In my mind's eye today, I can't look into that memory because it is too chilling. Literally it's like a coldness just came into the room as I am typing.

Soon MTDMI, my little brother, and I were in a car headed to Trafalga, a local fun center about seven miles from our house. My parents were out of town moving a trailer. The neighbor kids waved us off mournfully as their mom had said no. As we drove to Trafalga, I wrestled with what to do. I came up with a plan.

MTDMI bought our wristbands and then as the band was on my wrist and my brother's, I suddenly remembered I'd left my bag in the car. MTDMI came with me while my brother scampered inside to start the fun. In those days, kids were more free to wander, the idea or concept that a pedophile was lurking didn't occur to us. We didn't even know that word. And I say this bitterly, because I'd brought one with me. In that time, in our idealistic community, kids had free reign. Even at a public swimming place the only fear was drowning.

As we walked to his car he invited me to sit inside. The car had dark tinted windows, which gave him the opportunity to have "private time" with me, even if we were on an errand to go buy food, which was a frequent thing he did when coming to town. I'd go with him to pick the food, and this of course made me more aware of what he "provided" to my family.

This time, however, as we sat in the car, I kept the door open. He said to close it. I just sat there. He reached over to close the door and I put my foot outside. The door attempted to shut on my leg, which created the only visible bruise I'd ever gotten in our time together.

"What we did...wrong. I'm going to tell," I muttered to the floor of his car. In a calm tone he told me the consequences. The cool tech car he had chimed in, "The door is ajar." I wasn't really listening. I saw my neighbor girl and choked on the thought of what "we" did happening to her.

I was never allowed to raise my voice. Ever. It was never allowed for a kid to do so. I'd seen my sister do so to my mom, my mom to her, but it was ugly, and it was forbidden. My grandparents always forgave my sister these outbursts, but never my mom. Yelling meant you're out of control.

That summer day, I yelled. Okay, not really. I raised my voice in a not-sweet, un-kind, and un-thoughtful way. I said no. I told him if he was home when we got home, I'd go to the neighbor and tell her. It was an empty threat, but I think he wasn't totally sure. As I got out of the car, I did another big no-no. I slammed the car door. Hard.

I walked away and realized I had wet my pants. I had been so bad. I yelled, and I slammed his car door.

My brother asked where MTDMI was. I told him he got a page, that was how fancy rich people communicated back then, and he had to go back to California. As my brother played, I sat in the water. I felt sick. I just sat there.

My brother wasn't too impressed that we were miles from home and had to walk back dangling our wet suits to our sides, but eventually someone we knew gave us a ride. I lied, saying that I'd spent the bus money on treats. My brother, who was three years younger than me, just looked at me, puzzled. There had been no treats because MTDMI had left. No treats indeed.

The moment that I could have said the truth of why MTDMI had left passed, so I didn't say anything. Evidently, MTDMI told a story that made sense to my parents. I wasn't really asked much, as my lying was in the form of silence. I wasn't good at saying lies. I had just learned how to live with them.

Months passed and there were no visits from MTDMI. My siblings mentioned him. They missed him, the treats, the rides in his cool car that talked, and with the combo that only I had. I told my brother the combo, the brother that was into drugs. I imagined that he would steal MTDMI's money and that made me happy.

On July 22nd, 1987, MTDMI came to town after several months of distance. My sister was getting married, and he told my mom and dad that he needed to talk to them. My mom was in the frantic state of a wedding the next day. MTDMI sat down and talked with her about his history with relationships and his desire to settle down. He spoke of my positive traits. My mom did not understand that he was asking to marry her thirteen-year-old daughter. She was busy putting items together for the reception. He didn't clearly state to her his intentions.

After the wedding, he was more articulate with my dad. Dad was clear, "Leave now if you want to be whole. Remain and be castrated."

My parents didn't know that he had already acted out his physical desires. How could a parent imagine such an ugly thing? After all, I was "fine" as I always had been. All I remember from that was their shock and disgust. I cherished that my dad would castrate him. I still get a chuckle thinking about that.

The abuse had ended. MTDMI would never again spend time with me. My father is a big man, not prone to violence, yet no one had any doubt that MTDMI was not to be in our home. As the physical violations had ended the process, the path to healing was just beginning. It would be a long road and I started it with maintaining silence.

My parents had us kids in karate for years so we could protect ourselves. An interesting irony now is I could have really hurt MTDMI, but we had been told by our Sensei to never hurt anyone unless they were hurting us. I didn't understand that I was being hurt more deeply than the bruises I regularly got in his class. He encouraged the boys to be hard on me and he would taunt me for being a girl. He deeply resented my female presence in his DoJo. Just before writing this book, it came to light that he had molested several girls. It makes me sick to realize yet another molester to which I was so close. As the first female in his DoJo, I naturally asked the question if I paved the way to have girls in his influence. But then I have to remind myself the answer is no, because it is 100% the fault of the molester. Yet, his treatment of me highlights that abusers lack respect for others.

I was in the eighth grade the first year that I hadn't had MTDMI in my life. I was like most junior high kids: insecure, self-conscious, and exploring the bounds of my own power. There was a ramp at our school, and when you walked up the ramp, your bum kind of stuck out. Some boys thought it would be funny to run by the girls and smack their bottoms as they sped by. This spread through the school, we girls had to watch out! There were no stairs, so some girls would run up the ramp to avoid being smacked, and then giggle at the top. I was resentful that I would have to run to not be touched. No way would I be smacked. I prepared my response: each time I walked up the ramp I clenched my fist, rehearsing in my mind which foot would pivot, and how I would hold the impact of the blow. I heard the boy coming, forewarned by the other girls' reactions to his bum-smacks. As his hand brushed upon my bum, my fist met his nose. He fell flat, hitting his head with a thud on the ground. Everyone stopped. I was relieved I hadn't killed him. I punched that boy not with the rage of a fourteen-year-old girl protecting the sanctity of her bum, but with the strength of a girl who'd had enough. He had a broken nose and got a possible concussion. I was taken to the principal's office; I was in big trouble.

My mom is a warrior. She is tough. She drove Dad's other truck and her trucker's handle is "The Lady." I've seen her go toe-to-toe with big burly men and also laugh with bikers. She taught me etiquette and to see others with an eye of love. And as I sat there wringing my hands, I was scared to death. Mom came over to me, heard what happened, talked to the school administrators, and asked them one simple question, "Are you saying my daughter is in trouble for defending herself, something you didn't do?" I was released from teenage doom with my mom congratulating me for protecting myself.

Now I had two pieces of information: Dad was capable of castration and Mom was okay with me punching would-be bum assailants.

Chapter 6

From Victim to Survivor

"My attacker told me many times that I had better commit suicide, because that would be a lot easier to deal with than if he ever got me alone again. He threatened to kill my family members if I told. I was just thirteen. This boy had me on eggshells all the way from age 13 to 25, when I moved away to the east coast, and I was so embarrassed and ashamed of what he did to me."
–Josephine Ackman Franco #metoo

Dictionary definition of victim:

vic·tim (noun)
one that is subjected to oppression, hardship, or mistreatment; one that is tricked or duped.[5]

The MTDMI who trespassed on my soul definitely tried to "trick" me, or to "dupe" me. Since I didn't have any physical bruising, I thought these things were okay because of how my mind had been

---

5   Meriam-Webster Dictionary, s.v. "Shame," accessed July 2018, https://www.meriam-webster.com/dictionary/shame

messed with. The closer we are to the trespassers that abuse us, the more we are psychologically tricked, duped, and preyed upon. If it's an uncle, grandparent, cousin, sister, dad, these people that we interact with regularly, the easier it is to be psychologically injured.

Staying a victim is not a place that we can thrive. If I had a cut that scabbed over, but I kept picking at the scab, not only will it take longer for that cut to heal, but I also increase my chances of getting a scar. The longer we stay in the victim stage, the harder it is to go to a place where the abuser is not in control.

The pain of a victim is not something to be taken lightly. We need to recognize that a victim is in the middle of processing many emotions, thoughts, and sorting out truth from lies. Once the abuse stops, that doesn't mean that suddenly everything is now okay.

Tool #2: Recognize the stages of grief

A victim moves to a survivor through the stages of grief. Recognizing which step we are in is powerful. Each victim can take as little or as long as they are going to take. Don't bury the emotions. Deal with them. If you are a victim, doing the mental work that will get you through each of these phases will help you bring these emotions from pulsing in your heart, poisoning your body, up to dealing with it clearly in your mind.

Stages of grief include: denial and isolation, anger, bargaining, depression, and acceptance. Some of these overlap, but to get to the other side of grief, most people pass through all of these steps to some degree. Denying the reality of the violation that has occurred will cause a victim to feel isolated, confused, and unsure where to turn or what to do next. Once recognition of the abuse occurs, the victim feels anger at the abuser and also at those who covered it up.

Once steeped in anger, the victim typically bargains with themselves, asking the "if only" questions as to how things could have turned out differently. How could all of this been avoided, or what could have been done to prevent the abuse, to have been stronger, to have had more courage? Obviously, these are difficult questions and often self-defeating. This is where it is imperative that victims seek God's help and to ask Him to take their pain away. Once the pain subsides enough, the victim can begin to come to terms with what happened, accept it, and move beyond it.

Before reaching acceptance, however, victims will typically experience some level of depression. Dealing with such trauma, even if not physical, is not easy mentally or psychologically for anyone, and physical abuse can make the healing process more difficult. It's important to understand that most everyone has had a season of depression in his or her life, if not a chemical depression to work through. If you are a victim, create skills for dealing and coping with depression. Maybe in the middle of a depression, it's not comforting to know that depression is something millions of people have gone through, but as I'm walking down the street, it kind of helps me to know.

It's funny how we may be severely depressed and when someone says, "How are you?" we're like "Good, thanks, how are you?" I think it's healthy to tell people that we're struggling with depression, not to give us a pass in life, but to put a course of action in place. Feelings don't necessarily go away. They may diminish in time, but as long as we keep picking at them, like scabs, they are going to stay there and fester.

As a victim, getting to the acceptance stage allows you to move into survivor mode. This is realizing that the abuse happened but moving on with dignity and grace. We can understand that, unfortunately, it's something that happened. Now it's time for you to pass through grief, heal, and move on with living the life you were meant to live, that God meant you to live. I will go over some tools that I used later in this chapter.

So often we think the stages of grief are associated with death or the loss of a relationship. But isn't it a death of innocence? Isn't it a loss of a relationship with who you used to be? As a society, I believe that collectively we are in the anger stage, because we've only recently left the denial stage. We didn't talk about sexual assault, most of us didn't believe it was a problem, or we excused the abuser and blamed the victim. We are mad now that the curtain has been lifted on the societal problem of sexual abuse. Anger is such an easy place to stay, and it scares me that our society may never evolve from this stage. Although it is good to expose the guilty, innocent men are also being torn down and castigated, becoming collateral damage in a frenzy to elevate women above men. As we move into the bargaining stage, we may even slide backward and begin making excuses for abusers again, most likely because those abusers were once the victims. I believe the only way to achieve lasting healing as a society is to promote mutual love, and a part of that mutual love is to forgive and move on.

I believe that God is an essential piece of this cycle, and I know that some people may look at that as hate speech or small minded, but to me God is such an integral part of moving my anger from constantly pulsing through my body up to my mind where I can cope with it in a healthy way. God is augmenting the way I think, filtering what emotions I let through, and that is such an essential part of moving that hateful emotion outside of us. Once that hate is removed, we can more clearly see the holes that are in us. The loss. The loss of innocence. We can then focus on fixing us.

Although MTDMI was no longer in my life, I maintained my secret all through that next year. Roughly thirteen months after MTDMI had been banished we moved to a new town five hours south for an internship my mom was doing to complete her goal of earning a college degree. She had taken a college class here and there over the years—and always seemed to take finals pregnant with one of us five kids. My parents scrimped and saved to pay tuition.

I am sure that on this drive, her mind was full of her new responsibilities at leading her first class, the stress of pulling her two kids into a different school, moving and all those logistics, one daughter recently married, and two sons had moved out. A new chapter began as she went from five kids to two at home. I am sure she saw this as a time that she could pursue her goal of finishing her education so she could get better employment opportunities. After all, I was responsible and helpful to a fault. While it was a new beginning for her, I too saw it as new beginning.

I decided to tell my mom my part. I felt immense guilt and shame, and I was sure that my mom would be disappointed in me. I did have the hope that my parents, judging from the castration comments and the bum incident, would blame MTDMI more than me. I was ready for my punishment.

Now as a mother, I have wondered how hideously shocking it must be to hear from your daughter that a friend had mutilated your trust by violating your child.

When I arrived in Blanding, Utah, there was this poignant moment of putting my feet down on the gravel of our new home and realizing I had a new start. I am so grateful that through my mom's horror, and my mom talking to my dad in a phone booth expressing her anger, I came to understand that they did not blame me. Their trust and acceptance of me placed me in a safe place to begin to process the abuse.

Tool #3: Understand accountability, blame, and responsibility

There's a difference between accountability, blame, and responsibility. I was not accountable for MTDMI's vile actions. I was not accountable for him twisting my thoughts and emotions into thinking I was somehow responsible for him choosing to trespass on my body. The perpetrator causes 100% of rapes, assault, and molestations. I understand that the lines between accountability, blame, and responsibility can get a little foggy, but I will continue to separate them.

Accountability: When you as the victim take back control, you begin to understand that accountability rests with the one who did the wrong, not on the person wronged. As for God, responsibility and accountability will rest with the trespasser, no matter what he convinced the victim of and even if they fool the law. God judges and His judgments are just. And that is a peaceful thing to know, both for the victim and the victim-turned-abuser. God works it all out.

Blame: Blame is not taking accountability, it treats accountability as though it can be passed around. It can't. Society may say the victim is to blame for where they were and what they were wearing, but society is so wrong on this point. When a sexual act is perpetrated on another person without his informed consent, meaning full understanding and willful participation, this is assault and battery. Exposure to pornography, touching of the body, even grabbing another person's arm and not letting go, communicates a threat and therefore is an assault on that person (and the physical harm done is battery). Children are too young to offer up informed consent to any of these behaviors. The judgment of our legal system and society are flawed when asking the victim if she "was asking for it."

Responsibility: If you can see that your situation isn't okay, it isn't as much about how you got there as much as how you get out. I know 100% it is MTDMI's fault that he molested my body, but now it's my responsibility not to communicate that I accepted it. I had to stand up for me at some point.

After the abuse ended, it was now my responsibility to move me from a victim to a survivor. I couldn't give MTDMI anymore control over my life, anymore of my time. I was responsible for fixing my broken parts so that I wouldn't turn from victim to abuser.

When we have something awful that we've been chewing and gnawing on, we can either swallow and choke on it, or we can spit it out. If an abuser forced it in your mouth, that's something she is accountable for, but you still have the choice of spitting it out and handing it to God. If you found it on the ground and put it in your own mouth, then learn your lesson and spit it out. If we make the mistake, or someone makes a sin upon us, we don't have to keep or dwell on that. That's the greatest lie Satan tells, but the truth is we don't have to keep everything that happens to us. Give it to Jesus Christ whose balm of Gilead heals all.

I know a victim may somehow get a message that if something bad has happened to him, then it's on him. If this is the case, then there was some miscommunication between God and that victim. Maybe the teacher or preacher didn't correctly understand God's doctrine. We are not accountable for someone else's choices. We can only fix ourselves, and we are responsible for fixing us. MTDMI does not have the power to control the outcome of my life. When I was a child, he had a lot of power over my life, thus the evilness of the act. But as I have grown, I've been able to take that power back.

You can't have that clarity and continue chewing on an angry bone and vengefulness. You also can't have that clarity and be chewing on a responsibility to fix the violator. Eventually, you need to release both of these tendencies, forgive, and move on with your life.

To paint MTDMI as 100% evil is not accurate, although in my recovery it was what I needed to do. As I grew up, I began to realize that MTDMI had once been a child and a young man. Things happened that led him to make his choices. And now I can understand that because he didn't fix his broken soul, he perpetuated the cycle of violence. But it ended with him because I chose to let go of him. He would love to imagine that I still think about him. But he isn't important to me, because I have found other things that are more important.

My story is that I was a victim of sexual abuse and now, because I have been there, I am an advocate of strength and healing for others, for you. To understand who is at fault, sometimes those lines are blurred. He caused it, but I still have to figure out my own baggage. Otherwise, he holds all of the power.

As idealistic as it may be, I have been less judgmental because of the things that happened to me. Because I am not judging, I can be kinder. And because I am kind, I have had the opportunity to meet many wonderful, amazing people. And because I get to meet so many wonderful people, my perspective on the world has changed to where I believe humanity is basically good.

As I stepped onto the gravel of our new home, in the town of Blanding, I decided this would be where I would find the spice of life. The lightness that came from unloading all of my secrets, and the relief I felt that my parents at least mostly blamed MTDMI (note: they fully blamed him, my own thoughts were too twisted to fully comprehend that yet) made me truly believe that here was where I could be happy.

Then I attended the first day of my new school.

Chapter 7

Moving

"Your life is a movie. You are the main character. You say your scripts and act to your lines. Of course you do your lines in each scene. There is a hidden camera and a director who you can ask for help anytime up above."
-Diana Rose Morcilla

THE FIRST DAY AT MY new school I mustered up an incredible show of confidence. I stood up straight. I tried to look people in the eye when I talked to them. I tried not to be a dork. Things were going pretty well until I was asked to introduce myself in front of the class. Unfortunately, sometimes kids will be kids. When I stood in front of that class and said my name, everyone laughed. They didn't just laugh in that class; they pointed and laughed at me all day. I thought I knew why—I really *was* that ugly and dumb. The kids in Blanding hadn't been gradually broken into what was so absolutely awful about me like they had been back home. In Blanding, they got the shock diet: they saw me for exactly what I was. And they laughed, pointing at me and saying my name.

On the way home that day, feeling completely broken, I said what they said, mumbling my name. I said it again. Suddenly, I heard my name in a new way—the same way those kids had heard it: Leta Maughan. "Lead-'em-On." Great. *A streetwalker name!* Even my name mocked me. And I listened. I got the message. I'd tried to hide my dorkiness, and I'd failed. With their version of my name, they had something concrete of which to make fun. But their words were not nearly as damaging as the ones that were reinforced in my own mind, and it was all too much. I'd hoped for a new start, I'd hoped for something and instead I found all my worst thoughts about myself confirmed and that my name was now like the name of a porn star. I must really be bad.

Mom and Dad were horrified that they had accidently given me a whore name. But my mom had a plan for how I could change it all. Her plan, though well intentioned, is a good example of how adults and teenagers don't see problems in the same way. To me, my life was over. To my mom, I simply had to go to school the next day and introduce myself as "Frances" (my middle name). Of course, she reasoned, if I went to school as Frances, all the kids would immediately apologize for mocking me and respectfully call me Frances from then on.

I was right about one thing. Moving to Blanding really did change everything. I knew I would have to go to school the next day—there was no way my parents were going to let me quit and move to the hinterland of Alaska! And then, as I lay alone in my bedroom believing all those negative things, something whispered to me, pushing through the spiral of self-hatred.

Not long before that day I had begun to pray—uttering my own thoughts to the God in whom I believed. I believed in *Him*, but I didn't believe He cared for me as an individual. After all, I had proof! Life was hard, it hurt, and people could be cruel! From my perspective now, I can see He was always there—my pain is what had pushed Him out. But back then, I questioned. Something inside was asking me, demanding an answer. What did I mean to Him? What did *I* mean?

So that night after my first day at San Juan High School, I lay there in the darkness and told God everything He had messed up for me. I looked up bitterly. Then an astonishing thought occurred to me. I had to decide what Leta Maughan meant. I had to practice a new way of thinking. This was almost Joan of Arc talk. Maybe I was crazy. *Practice a new way of thinking?*

At that moment, a powerful thought came into my mind: *Everyone in this room loves me.* I hadn't read it in a book. No self-help guru put it there. It came as pure truth, whispered by a loving God. I said it over and over and over again, all alone in my room, speaking it quietly until sleep finally overtook me.

Before I walked into class the next morning, a voice inside of me reminded me of what I now knew. I said to myself, *Everyone in this room loves me.* How could everyone love me? Suddenly I felt an intense love from my Father in Heaven. It was so clear: He loved everyone. He loved me completely. And with that, so much was possible.

Everyone in this room loves me. Everyone (breath) in this (breath) room. Loves. Me. I opened the door, and seeing the faces made me smile. They were smiling—at me. With borrowed bravado, I said, "Leta Maughan here!" They laughed, just as they had the day before—but this time it felt like they were laughing *with* me, not *at* me.

It may sound miraculous, and to me it was. That experience transformed how I saw the world and how the world saw me. There was no makeover. There was no wardrobe change. There was no public announcement. There was no dance scene where my awkwardness was whisked away, leaving me suddenly cute. I still had blotchy skin. I still had a missing front tooth and two very large, temporary, gray-streaked teeth. I still had scar tissue. I still wore the same hand-me-downs. I still lived on the corner lot of the trailer court by the stump. In actuality, though, there *was* a makeover, and it was a significant one: My thought process was made over.

Instead of focusing on what was wrong with me, I started to see what was right. Everything was as it had been the day before, but everything had changed because I had changed the thoughts in my own head.

Two weeks later, at a school dance in the cafeteria-turned-dance-hall, a boy walked up to me and asked me to be his girlfriend. It was cute, awkward, and sweet in the first-romance kind of way. Eric was a tenth grader and I was a freshman.

"Okay," I said, "But I have some rules. You can hold my hand and carry my books, but you can only hug me when I say you can and not for too long."

"Okay," he agreed respectfully.

"Also, you can't kiss me."

"How long until I can kiss you?"

"The summer before my senior year." That time table hadn't actually been thought out before, but the idea of waiting three years before moving to that next physical step felt comfortable to me.

And guess what? That hormone-filled teenage boy waited. He waited until I was ready, and he was my first kiss of consent the summer before my senior year of high school. Now, we were in a small school, and when word got out that we'd been dating for "so long" without kissing, because in a small-town school six weeks is a long-term relationship, he was teased. But he still respected me and my boundaries enough that he waited those three years. We were always together and became such good friends.

Speaking in terms of broad generalizations, there are two ways that victims of sexual abuse tend to go: 1) extremely promiscuous or 2) extremely conservative. Once their boundaries are violated, victims often don't understand how to re-establish them. They either don't re-establish them at all, then people are like, "See? She is promiscuous. It wasn't his fault." Or, they push those boundaries in so deep and often become very cynical about physical affection and love. I became the latter. I was very controlling, but sweet Eric respected me, the young woman in me.

Eric respected any boundary that I put in place. When he first told me he loved me, I told him that we were too young to use that word or to understand it. Remember, MTDMI had also claimed to love me. So I told Eric that he could say "wuv" instead of love, because I was a huge *Princess Bride* fan. ("Mawage. Mawage is what bwings us togeder today...to cewebwate wuv, twue wuv...") Eric was the boy that I needed to restore my faith in males. Whenever I hear stories of "boys will be boys," I remember Eric, and I know that we can hold our youth to high standards.

Tool #4: Focus on your thoughts and words

Before that fateful morning when I decided that everyone loved me, I had made myself the victim because I saw myself as the victim. Life events reinforced how I felt and became who I was. But I was not what I thought. None of us are what we think—we are more than we know. My whole world was different. I could see that now.

You have that same power. If you believe you can walk on fire, you can. (I have, actually, and it was awesome!) If you believe you have no self-control, you will eat a pan full of brownies. If you believe you are beautiful, you are. We can think only what we are willing to think. If you open your heart to God and take control of your thoughts, you take control of your life.

Just like so many other things in life, this is easier said than done. We resist learning new things. Change, even good change, is uncomfortable, and even with good intentions we forget to follow through. Those negative habits are ingrained in us. To counteract this, we have to make a very deliberate effort and plan time in our schedules so that our new thoughts will be implemented and have a chance to become part of our brain patterning.

We take the time to reach out to others in loving, thoughtful ways. We even pray for them in times of illness or tragedy. But when it comes to ourselves, we tend to be neglectful. We understand that the words we use with others have power—power to help, hurt, build, or destroy. But we seem to ignore that fact when dealing with our own preprogrammed self-criticism. We should be spending time reaching out to ourselves in loving, thoughtful ways, praying for ourselves and our success, as it were, regardless of whether we define prayer as a petition to God or an earnest request or wish.

We can't control the ideas to which we'll be exposed, but we don't have to buy into them once we know better. In other words, we don't have to live with and accept the ideas that have been holding us back.

Tool #5: Know how to forgive and be free

God has asked us to forgive. The idea that you could forgive someone who has trespassed your physical body is an emotionally-charged concept. Forgiveness, ultimately, is not for the abuser. The reason I am so glad that I have forgiven is not to liberate MTDMI from responsibility. It is to liberate responsibility from me. Forgiveness breaks the chains of bitterness.

Sometimes we think forgiveness means liberating the violator from responsibility. But really, forgiveness is between me and God. It's saying to MTDMI that I release him from owning me, and I release my responsibility to fix you. I recognize that you are a Son of God, and I release you to God to fix. I don't carry around what he did to me, and I don't carry around the responsibility of doing something about it.

I can't take legal justice into my hands, but I do not have to be around MTDMI. If I could press charges this many years later and prove he did what he did, then I would, because his actions deserve consequences. Vengeance? No. Some people use the justice system for vengeance, and I'm not going to judge those people who do. I am glad, however, that my dad didn't shoot MTDMI with a shotgun, because then my dad would be in jail. Consequences should follow actions. But we don't need to act out in anger. Of course, most of us do, me included, but generally the angry reaction isn't the right one.

Years later, MTDMI reached out to my brother Lance. MTDMI took advantage of Lance's goodness and gave him a letter for me.

MTDMI's message was that he had been cheated out of his ideal partner in life. He has no remorse. He still takes no accountability for his actions. That proves that I needed to forgive him to free him from my life. There's nothing I can do to fix him or make him understand that what he did was wrong. And since he is a sociopath, I do not want him in charge of my recovery.

A close friend of mine reached out to me with her story. As a teenager, she was raped on a date. That was an extremely difficult thing for her to work through, but through God, she was eventually able to let go of that baggage. Years later, that boy approached her, now with his wife. He apologized for his actions and asked for her forgiveness.

She said it was amazing to her that she could so readily say yes, because she had forgiven him years ago. Her forgiveness wasn't dependent on him or his actions or inactions. And when he was ready, he was able to get his crap together and, through God, become a better person. She said his apology wasn't required for her to get to the place of happiness that she is currently in. His apology was nice, but it wasn't anything that she needed.

It's wonderful they could have that resolution, but this is not a typical story. Not everyone gets that closure. Most people don't take accountability. Thus, don't give the perpetrator power over your happiness. Hasn't he already taken enough? Don't you deserve to not base your future joy and happiness on her attitude?

The truth of the matter is that there are a lot of ugly things that happen in our world, and they have been happening for a very long time. I'm not so naive to preach that if we were all a little less judgmental then the bad people in the world would suddenly have a desire to stop their evil acts and go open a bakery.

But I do know, that for individual victims, staying in a place of anger is further self-harm, additional self-victimization. You need to go through the anger and the grief and to process these things. There are some things that are so ugly, so horrible that after you've chewed it long enough to know what it is, just spit it out. For me, that means handing it to God. I label all the bad things as grit, and I know that if I swallow it that it will make my digestive system all in tangles. Once I've chewed all the lessons out, I spit it out and give it to God.

But, as that young girl in Blanding, I decided it was either death or going forward. I decided to go forward. That led to the creation of Happy Town. And no, that isn't some crazy LSD thing.

Chapter 8

Journey to Happy Town

"I told my uncle I was going to tell my father. He actually stopped. When he finally left our home, my hell began, as I didn't feel safe with anyone and the shame consumed me for a long time."
–Yolanda #metoo

IF YOU WERE TO ASK me as a kid what I wanted to be when I grew up, I would have said a special education teacher, because that's what my mom was. My mom said if I was a teacher then I would have job security and be doing something meaningful. But you know what I really wanted? I wanted to be happy.

Because my dad was a truck driver, I had many hours of staring out the window looking at road signs. I love road signs. I have them all over my house. I can't really explain the nostalgia I have for watching those white lines whiz by.

I'd look out the window and see towns and I'd imagine the people that live there and what their lives were like. I'd always ask myself, "Are they happy?" Sometimes I'd see people that were happy, sometimes people that were sad. Sometimes I'd see people in crappy towns with crappy houses and little crappy yards, and I'd watch them laughing and know they really were happy. I learned that it wasn't circumstances that made you happy. Abused kids learn quickly how to read body language. We understand true emotions, because we know that anger meant getting hurt and happy meant things would be okay for a while. We can tell when we see someone who is happy. And, when I saw real happiness, I would wonder how it happened.

Tool #6: Make the journey to Happy Town

I began to create a metaphor in my life. It's pretty straightforward and simple, and has been used a lot. There is a mountain we need to climb, and at the top of this mountain is Happy Town. All of us at some point in life have been at the bottom. One person's bottom may be darker and lower than another's bottom, but each of us have been at the bottom. No one lands at the top of the mountain. You might think you're at the top, or you might think you're higher than other people because of your circumstances in life, but there is always something above you for which you are reaching.

Staying put isn't an option, because there's always something trying to pull you down. The forces that want to pull you down are just the realities of life. How you think, the way you treat other people, your perceptions—all will either pull you down or give you the will to push you up.

When you're hiking, it's going to burn your calf muscles. But you just keep moving one more step, one more step. Then you get smacked by a wayward branch and fall on your butt. Sometimes the path is so steep you are crawling up it, fingernails scratching into the sides. My analogy will sometimes switch between hiking or driving up the mountain but moving toward Happy Town is always the end goal. And it's not just the destination, it's about learning to enjoy the climb in your journey.

The great thing about going up the mountain is that the higher you get, the greater your vista. I enjoy hiking. I like to stop and take in the view along the way, which works more as a cover to catch my breath.

What's amazing is that sometimes your view from twenty feet up is vastly different than just ten feet up. And as you're hiking, the vista just gets better and better. You have to get out of the mud dump first though.

So as I sat in my dad's truck or when I looked around my neighborhood, I'd see these people and some of them were happy and some of them were not and I'd think, "Maybe I could just work on being a person that's actually happier."

You can only lay at your rock bottom for so long. I have seen people who take the art of self-pity to a whole new level of skill. But my theory is that if you can talk about it, or if you can recognize it for what it is, then you're at a stage where you can do something about it. You can take action.

You can look at the top of the mountain and say, "I want to be there so bad! I want to get to the top! I want to be at Happy Town." But nobody, *not even God,* can make you decide to start up the mountain. Nobody can make you work on you. You can talk to people until your throat is dry, you can talk until you're out of air, but until you take accountability for your feelings, you will stay a victim. You will stay a victim until you decide to be different.

"The world has rarely treated happiness as a state worthy of serious respect, and yet, if we see someone who, in spite of life's adversities, is happy a good deal of the time, we should recognize that we are looking at spiritual achievement—and one worth aspiring to."[6]

This is one of my favorite quotes and hangs on my bedroom mirror. Another that I heard as a young adult that has always been in front of me is another by Charles R. Swindoll:

> *"The longer I live, the more I realize the impact of attitude on life. Attitude is more important than the past, than education, than money, than circumstances, than failures, than success, than what other people think or say or do. It is more*

---

6 Nathaniel Brandon PHD, *Taking Responsibility: Self Reliance and the Accountable Life* (Simon & Schuster, 1997) 10

important than appearance, giftedness or skill. It will make or break a company…a home… The remarkable thing is we have a choice every day regarding the attitude we will embrace for that day. We cannot change the inevitable. The only thing we can do is play on the string we have, and that is our attitude…I am convinced that life is 10% what happens to me and 90% how I react to it. And so it is with you…we are in charge of our attitudes."

Like on any journey there are pit stops, there are times that you can take a break. I have a girlfriend that I call when I'm frustrated, and I need to say, "This is what happened. Am I being crazy? Or are they crazy? Or am I being crazy on them?" She's a good friend who will tell me that either they are crazy, or that I need to do better. I believe good friends actually tell us when we can do better.

If you can see that what you have isn't normal, then it's up to you to change it. I wish there was a magic bullet, but there just comes a point where you say enough is enough. At some point that moment clicks that you can imagine things different.

It is natural and normal to be sad that you were molested, raped, or abused. But that does not take away from the fact that you now have to deal with what has happened to you. The stage of moving from victim to survivor is where the view gets a little better. We can see the pit a little differently because of perspective, and because our muscles and coping skills are getting stronger.

I'm a Survivor

sur·vi·vor

sər'vīvər

1. to remain alive or in existence

2. to continue to function[7]

---

7 Meriam-Webster Dictionary, s.v. "Survivor," accessed July 2018, https://www.merriam-webster.com/dictionary/survivor

You become a survivor when you are ready to move on from being a victim, when you can fully enter into the acceptance stage of the stages of grief. I always imagine a survivor coming out of a forest, caked in blood, looking more like a soldier or plane crash victim. I didn't have anyone coaching me through these stages, I think it would have shortened my recovery time if I had.

Once I started getting a handle on first what had happened—that it was wrong—and processing those different steps, I mourned it. I felt the guilt, the anger, I went through those different stages, even though it wasn't so clearly defined. As you're reading this you may say to yourself, "Okay, am I in the victim status? Am I in denial? Do I believe the abuser's excuses and rationalizations? Or, am I just angry?" If these are your questions, then I strongly encourage you to analyze your thinking processes, your words, and even your actions to determine where you are in your path to get to the top of your mountain, to *your* Happy Town. Maybe you have further to go, so it is my hope that this book will help you get there, and more efficiently than it took me.

In my *Hotness* book, I talk about my grandmother's frequent attacks on my looks as a child. She would consistently tell me how ugly I was, and that I would never be married. Or if I were married, it wouldn't be until later in life when a man's wife had died, and he would need help raising his kids. You know, just the normal things grandmas say.

Fortunately, I never received the message in my religion that I was damaged. I know there are other people who have, but I never got the message that I was damaged goods. Because I believed in the Atonement of Jesus Christ, I believed that Christ came and not only suffered for my sins, but He could take away the shame and guilt I felt thinking of all the things I should have done. Importantly, I also learned that I did not sin when the abuse happened, but this took some time to realize. As an adult, I can now recognize that as the bargaining stage: I should have fought back, I should have said something earlier, I should have... But, I didn't.

I found a new destination other than guilt and anger because I saw other happy people. The risk is when hideous things happen, you assume it's just you, that no one else could possibly understand. It's kind of minimizing. After that year in Blanding, we moved back to our home in Provo, the one with the dip in which cars would get stuck. There were some really big houses not far away from mine, which was great for my brothers and me. This nicer neighborhood was always in need of kids to shovel the Utah snows, rake the fall leaves, and to my delight, I had the reputation of being the best house cleaner. I had a steady stream of work.

One day while taking a break from cleaning to eat my lunch, the lady of the house started talking to me. She never came out and said it, but I realized she had been sexually assaulted in some way. As her eyes searched mine, she said I could make a great life for myself. I knew she knew. At first, I felt hot with embarrassment, but she reached her hand across the table, grasped mine and told me I was of value. I was loved, and my life would be amazing, and to work to make it that way. I understood work.

As I sat in her beautiful home noting her life of physical comforts, it hit me that if she, too, had experienced abuse and could have a great life, then so could I. I noticed how she laughed with her kids, she talked to them, she took moments to teach them and to teach me. I saw that when her husband came home he called out with affection for his wife. Her life was more than physical comforts, it was a happy life.

I learned other practical things about being a girl and a young woman from those in my neighborhood. It was another lady I cleaned for that casually mentioned that washing your hair with the pads of your fingers makes your hair feel better. Another lady generously offered to allow my family to use her washing machine. When she noticed that I had hand-me-down underwear from my brothers, she bought me some girly, flowery underwear, just so that I could feel pretty for myself.

That one of these neighbor ladies had experienced horrors opened my eyes, and her sensitivity to me made me feel seen. Seen not for what I could do, but just because of who I was. My relatives' voices became dulled in a chorus of angels singing around me, their voices sang of love for family and love for God. Since that night in Blanding, I could hear an echo in my own heart of my self worth. I had let MTDMI, and others that were broken, define the music in my head.

All of these people were a community around me, most were the kind of people to emulate and others were examples that taught me what not to be. I had a choice that I wasn't aware of for so long. Those that hurt me seemed the loudest, when now I look back I realize that I was literally surrounded by so much good. I just had to decide which examples I would follow.

Chapter 9

My Mission Story

"What I wish young girls would be assured today is that they are not alone and can seek help. We are worthy to be heard. We are worthy to be healed, and then we are worthy to be of HOPE to someone else." –Yolanda #metoo

I SPENT THE SUMMER AFTER high school working in the Grand Canyon. Then I began college at BYU with 18 credits. I was failing. My grandparents were deeply disappointed in me and expressed it. I was described as a failure at family gatherings. How embarrassed they were that I was failing school.

Maybe I was running away from my grandma and disappointed relatives, maybe I'd read too much Jack London, but I ran away to The Last Frontier, Alaska. Now, I can see I was still looking for something that made me special. If you had asked me then, the only thing I felt I had accomplished was that I had survived my childhood. Going to Alaska, the plan was to work for a year or so and save enough money to finish my education. I fell in love with a man I thought I was going to marry. One day, distressed over a series of family drama, I went out on a drive to clear my mind.

On the inlet of bay outside of Anchorage, I sat watching the tide, the birds. I pulled out my scriptures and read from the Book of Mormon that day, seeking answers. "But if ye will turn to the Lord with full purpose of heart, and put your trust in him, and serve him with all diligence of mind, if ye do this, he will, according to his own will and pleasure, deliver you out of bondage." (Mosiah 7:33)

It hit me. I hadn't really turned to God with full purpose. I was always asking Him to give me this or give me that. I stood up, brushed the dirt and leaves from my clothes, and knew what the next chapter of my life was going to be. I broke up with the boy and filled out my mission papers over the next week, which told my church that I wanted to serve a mission. I could be sent anywhere in the world and would serve for a period of eighteen months, possibly be asked to learn a language. Sending this application said I would go wherever I was sent. We don't pick where we go, we are assigned.

My bishop (the equivalent of my pastor) thought I was crazy to leave such a great guy. I told him to pray about it. He did. When my grandparents heard I wanted to leave, they called the bishop to tell him that I had been sexually active—how they viewed the abuse—and that I wasn't "clean" or "worthy" to serve a mission. It was a funny conversation, and possibly the first time I heard anyone disparage my grandparents. He discounted their comments and assured me that what an evil man had done had not tainted me in the least. My bishop signed my papers with a smile, shaking my hand and telling me I'd be a great missionary. He congratulated me in obeying the call and not letting his first impulse or others' opinions hold me back from going.

Missionaries or their families are expected to pay for the mission, which includes two years for boys and eighteen months for girls. I wrote a check leaving only $144 dollars in my account. This was money I had been saving for school. Being able to pay for my own mission made me feel that this was truly my gift back to God and to those with whom I would share His love.

I was twenty-one and ready to give gratitude to God. I received a call to serve an American Sign Language Mission. For so much of my life, I felt shame that I had fallen off a psychological cliff, that I couldn't cope with the things that happened to me. I scraped and clawed my way to the top of the edge of the cliff, and when I reached it, I wanted everyone to see that I was a functional human being.

I thought it was pretty awesome that I was functioning so well, but I was actually still in survivor mode. Almost in pride, I swore that I would *never* be at the bottom of that cliff looking up at Happy Town again.

My first area of service was in the Michigan, Lansing Mission. A lady told us her traumatic story of being molested in great detail. After hearing her story, and many others stories, many issues that I hadn't dealt with properly started coming up in my nightmares, things I look back on now as symptoms of the PTSD of which I hadn't yet been formally diagnosed.

I was really mad at myself. Here I was trying to do something good, and I couldn't get rid of my past. I would come to learn that anything that we don't deal with properly will come back again and again until we do. You see, in the Deaf culture, when language isn't available and a person is unable to communicate, it makes a ready victim. Many Deaf children do not know sufficient American Sign Language (ASL) to properly communicate.

I remember in one particular situation, a mother of four children disclosed to me that she had been molested. Although I didn't recognize it at the time, I was in the acceptance phase of grief. I could only acknowledge that the abuse had happened, but I wasn't at peace with it and I couldn't coach people on how to heal. This mother was telling me about her abuse through sign language, and she couldn't even look at me when she was signing. This was particularly heart wrenching because so much of sign language is about eye contact and facial expressions. She said she thought she was okay until the kids came, then she just didn't want to be with her husband anymore. As a twenty-one-year-old girl, I didn't know what to say to her.

It came to me to tell her that God understood, and that He would be there for her, and to trust Him. I'll never forget the look in her eye as she just stared at me, then signed, "You know?" I said yes. I said I was working on giving it to Him myself, but I believed it was going to work. I didn't recognize at the time that acceptance isn't having all the answers. It's deciding to find the path forward. I wanted to help her, and in that desire to ease her pain, my pain was less isolating. I wanted to be a ray of hope for her, and that felt fantastic.

That was my first taste of being an advocate, but that night I had nightmares. From then on, I started having quite a bit of nightmares. I had to throw myself into understanding the nature of God. For those of us that are raised with a certain understanding of God, sometimes it can be hard to reach that deep level of trust and understanding of His nature.

Trauma registers to our brain in a chemical response. When our minds have "cracks," unresolved pain acts out in odd ways. In our dream state, that is a "safe place" for the chemical reaction to leak, which is often why we have nightmares. You need to repair the leak.

Because I fell off that proverbial cliff and went all the way to the bottom, the consequences are two-fold. I am damaged psychologically and physically. Now, that doesn't mean that I can't have a great life. My soul was damaged, but my God has made that history into something with which I can love and serve. The physical scars are different than you would imagine, since MTDMI's abuse didn't leave bruises or blood. Because of his mental manipulation and grooming, I suppressed the light and feeling that told me MTDMI's actions were wrong. When you suppress emotions like that, your body physically holds onto it and will later bring it up.

We get sick for two reasons. First, our bodies are human. We are susceptible to germs, disease, injury—that's just part of being human.

Second, when the body's immune system gets low enough, a lot of illnesses will manifest. It's like driving a car with a flat tire on a bumpy road, eventually other things will break.

I do not believe that everyone who is sick falls under the umbrella I'm about to explain. Since I was molested year after year, I have physical consequences. It's interesting to look at my health history and see how the events interplayed with each other. I was repeatedly sick in junior high, so my mom took me to the doctor. He was the first one to tell me I had mononucleosis, or mono. A lot of people get mono and it's very contagious. Some people call it the kissing disease, because it can come from kissing. Once you have mono, you won't ever get it again, but that's knowledge I didn't have.

As Dr. Clayton, also in our church family, looked in my eyes and told me the diagnosis, he was crying, because he's a very tender-hearted man. Evidently, I had it pretty bad.

Mononucleosis is confirmed through a fairly simple blood test checking for antibodies. It makes you super tired, gives you swollen lymph nodes and sore throat, headaches, and affects the liver and spleen as your body tries to rid itself of the toxins backed up in the system. The first time I got mono I was maybe thirteen. I did not feel well for a long time. It's hard at this time to know if I ever got healthy.

When I was around sixteen, my parents' insurance changed and I had to go to a new doctor. I missed a semester of school because I was so sick. Without taking any blood work, this doctor told me that there is a switch in your head, and you just need to flip it on. She said that I was being lazy.

I took that phrase from her, an authority figure, and went home. "I am lazy," I told myself over and over again. The doctor didn't run blood tests that would have told her that because I'd had mono several times, that it had morphed into Epstein Barr Virus or EBV, named after the doctors who discovered the condition. Epstein Barr is a chronic form of mono, though not contagious like mono. It had now transformed in my body and was something I would have to deal with. Without the knowledge of what was really wrong, I just believed I was lazy and slept too much.

It kind of felt similar to some people's reactions to my sexual abuse. My ignorance of what was wrong with me didn't protect me from the consequences. I convinced myself that I was being lazy when really, I was out-running my body's capacity to recover. People can tell you to not be sad about abuse because "boys will be boys" and you're like oh, okay, I'm fine. So I went home and did what the doctor had told me to do and I tried to not be lazy, which was the same thing I had done about the abuse: I tried not to be sad about it. While I was blessed that a few people believed and supported me, many did not. It wasn't until I was able to label what was true or not with reference to the abuse that happened to me that I was able to come to terms with it.

Perhaps not surprisingly, in retrospect, my physical health and the abuse all mirrored each other. I didn't get blood tests done because I didn't know that was something I should be doing to monitor it. I would reprimand myself for being tired in the morning. I took a nap for too long once and prayed for forgiveness for being lazy. I had unknowingly given my power to this doctor.

Accordingly, on my mission, the PTSD and subsequent lack of sleep, cumulative stress, all began to increase exponentially. My throat swelled to where I couldn't really talk, but it was okay because I primarily used ASL. I went into a doctor and this doctor was asking me questions. Yeah, I'd lost muscle, and had this odd swelling in my abdomen. He took some blood work and then I left.

This doctor called me later and asked me to come in, but I told him that I was too busy with my humanitarian service. He told me I needed to come in anyways and I told him no. So he called the lady who acts as the mother figure to those of us out there serving and she called me and said that I really did need to go see the doctor. I went in, and the doctor told me I was very sick.

Huh?

You are very sick.

What?

You have been very sick for a long time. Truthfully, if a blood test had been taken, I would have never been sent out on a mission. I thank God no blood test was taken before I left on my mission.

A blessing of being on a mission was that I was under church coverage for my well-being. I was placed in counseling, which family finances had never permitted me to do previously. At first, I felt guilty that church funds were being used on me. The counselor told me that part of a mission is to find myself. I went to a counselor once a week for a few months. After the last appointment, my missionary companion bought me ice cream at Cold Stone Creamery. To this day, I associate Cold Stone Creamery with a very rich, good feeling. What an amazing way to find your true self, serving others. It worked, I found a new me, free of the burdens MTDMI placed on me.

It was in serving the people, and the counseling my church paid for me to receive, that really set my path. I had been suppressing so many things that they had eventually crippled me physically and spiritually. Prior to the mission, my coping strategy had been to ignore the past and reframe it as not really that bad. I had been trying to hike over fissures, failing to recognize the chasms that were breaking down my spirit. But going on a mission made me look at them and address the root causes of my physical issues.

I was sent home due to my health, but through the kindness of my church, they kept me on their insurance so that I could receive the care that I needed. I was told I would never be healthy again. I was only twenty-two years old.

Not anticipating that I would be coming home early, and not understanding just how sick I was, my parents put me on a mat in a spare room. A broom between two boxes acted as a closet where I hung my clothes.

So there I was, twenty-two years old, lying on a mat in a spare bedroom for months, reliving the announcement that I would never be healthy again. I had just had this amazing experience, being able to serve and love people and teach them about the light of the Gospel of Jesus Christ. And I'd had a taste of being an advocate for the first time. When everything else is out of your life, it is an opportunity to rebuild. When everything has been stripped away, we get to decide where to go. I got to choose, bit by bit, what to put back in.

The next time a doctor told me I would never be healthy again, I told him, "You don't know what my life purpose will be." I decided not to feel sorry for myself, to mold myself into something more.

My cute nieces and my brother were living with my parents at the time. They would ask me why I was sick and I'd tell them it was because I didn't eat my vegetables. The truth of why I was in that bed is because I was trying to hike too quickly over tough terrain. It's okay to slow down and really look at where you're going to put your feet. That uphill will only last so long until you get on the smooth trail again. You have to move forward, but it is a blessing to take it slow.

In our fast-paced world, we think it's a badge of honor to go fast. When we go on vacation and watch the sunrise or sunset, we may say, "Why don't we do this at home?" That's because we fill our lives so full of activity that we are flooding our brains with cortisol, which causes fight-or-flight reactions in our bodies. Take a moment to stop and just breathe. Put down your phone and have eyeball time with your loved ones. Sleep people, just sleep! If I get less than seven hours of sleep, I can feel my mental tools breaking down. That's when I know it's time to slow down.

I have a busy and demanding life. I have to go have blood tests done regularly to monitor my chronic autoimmune disease. One doctor thinks I don't actually have the lifestyle that I say I do. She thinks I'm sick in a bed all day long. But I've laced up my boots, I'm hiking to Happy Town.

I don't go around telling people that I have an autoimmune disease because I don't let it define me, but also a lot of people have a misconception that it's contagious. When I was seventeen I thought I was contagious. When Eric leaned in for that long-awaited first kiss, I told him, "Wait, I have mono, you might get sick."

"I'll take my chances," he said. Best teenage line ever.

I am a big fan of modern medicine, but there isn't anything that can cure my disease. The fact is that my blood just doesn't like to make as much oxygen as other people's blood. And I'm sure that you sell something that you think can fix it for me, but trust me on this, there's no cure.

Every morning when I wake up, I have a walking cane tucked to the side of my bed. It reminds me of a time when I needed that cane to walk, which was an improvement from the wheelchair I had been in (yup, we'll get to that story later). That walking cane is there as a reminder of the blessing I have now. I may not be able to sleep on my bad hip, which I affectionately call "my old lady parts," and when I awake in the morning, it whines a little. I see that walking cane and I am thankful because today I walk.

I also need to sleep longer than the average person, which is annoying because my husband is a morning person. If I get less than seven hours of sleep, things in my body start to break down. I thrive on eight hours, but I delight in nine. The sounds of nature, the sunlight creeping in my window and breakfast in bed is my favorite way to wake up. My awesome hubby brings me breakfast in bed often. Yeah, I know, I am so lucky. One morning he teased me, "People would think a powerhouse like you would be up!" I said they would be wrong as I turned over in the warm covers.

I thank God that I am so well. I also don't overcommit myself. I know I can only do so much. I know I have to work on my physical limitations and my mental limitations. These things together have taught me emotional empathy. The ability to look at others and imagine what they are going through has helped me love people.

Someone once asked if I could take it all away, would I? And I answered no, because I like who I am today. I wouldn't risk giving up this person, this person that had to crawl through so many obstacles to become who she is today. That may not make sense to someone who is angry. But I believe it when God says He works out all things for them that love the Lord. I believe He cumulates all things into something greater.

There is no greater gift that life can give you than liking who you are. I love that I'm a defender. I love that I have the wisdom and empathy that comes from all these different experiences.

Chapter 10

Life Just Doesn't Stop

*"My mission in life is not merely to survive, but to thrive; and
to do so with some passion, some compassion,
some humor, and some style." –Maya Angelou*

WHEN I WAS PREGNANT WITH my daughter, Ailsa, the pregnancy
was pretty difficult. My doctor noticed I was jumpy, then ended
up diagnosing me with PTSD. The physical toll that pregnancy took
on me was a lot and contributed to me being in a wheelchair several
years later.

When I was pregnant with my second daughter Katelynn, I went
to a different doctor and had myself reassessed. That doctor again diagnosed me with PTSD. We assumed this was because of the immense
physical pain from my past pregnancies. I realized I was in more of a
rest stop on my climb up the mountain, or my drive on the road of life.
I wasn't backtracking, but I wasn't moving up.

When I got myself formally evaluated, the therapist asked me how
long I'd had the PTSD symptoms. At first, I answered after my second
child or ninth pregnancy, then realized I should move it back to after
my first pregnancy. I then realized I needed to move it back further. It

was a hard day to realize I'd had PTSD symptoms for as long as I could remember, and that the nightmares were not about pregnancy, but the trauma of my childhood. It was hard to have someone tell me that my brain was basically seared.

It was traumatizing to realize that I have PTSD, which was a scar that came from the sexual abuse. I jump whenever I hear a loud or repetitive noise. As I was pregnant with Ailsa, I remember lying in bed one night, thinking "I could just let go." Hadn't I pushed hard enough, for long enough? I could just stop trying. Stop climbing. And I could just sit here on the side of this figurative road with a sign above me that said "Broken Down Woman."

I began compiling a pamphlet of all the reasons why I was broken and oh boy would I be justified. I would be so justified. I was so tired. I didn't sleep well because of the pain, and of course, I had the prospect of a newborn's sleep schedule to look forward to. I was really tired, and life just seemed so unfair. I'd finally gotten married to a really great guy, then we started having all these miscarriages and my body was hurting. It was just hard after hard after hard, and it just keeps going.

Life.

Just.

Doesn't.

Stop.

That night I laid in bed with my two-year-old son "cuddled" next to me in a twin bed. Cuddled of course is a loose term, because if you've ever had to sleep with a two-year-old, then you understand it's a lot more like kicking. We were in a twin because we were living with a saintly friend while my husband completed an internship for his career. I had my young son next to me, and my infant child inside of me, and God said, "Okay. But if you check out, who's going to raise your kids?"

God always knows what to say. Dang it.

At that moment, I could see the choice. I do believe that for most of us, with normal intelligence, that there is a moment when we choose life. I realized that I had climbed this far, but maybe I could climb at a slower pace right now.

There were many times when I looked at my son and have just been thankful he was in my life at that hard time. What if I hadn't had him? My husband is awesome, and I know that checking out would have been hard on him, but my son would have been fundamentally different if I had just stopped, prepared my placard, and held a "Broken Down Woman" sign above my head.

I believe there is a genetic disposition toward depression, anxiety, or PTSD, and there is enough research to back that up. But I have seen people start climbing again after insurmountable hard things that provided inspiration to me. And that helped me start climbing again. It's a very powerful coping tool to find someone who has gone through a similar situation and is doing well.

It isn't instant, it's a process. You may not even realize how much progress you have made until you stop for a moment and see the view. It is so much better, as gratitude fills your heart, because as hard as it was, it is so much better now. Others may be whizzing past you, hiking faster, but don't let that stop you from enjoying how far you've come. Take a drink of water, smile to yourself. See those other hikers below you? Encourage them. Shout out, "The view is even better up here!" Yodel if you want.

I am forever altered, for good and bad, because of what happened to me in my youth.

Tool #7: Pick your trajectory and drive your car

Back in the day, when I would drive around with my Dad, we had maps. On the map, you had to look and understand that route that you were driving to get to your correct destination. With the GPS, a lot of us don't understand the exact route, and we're just driving around hoping that we will get to the right place. Don't get me wrong, I love my GPS, but I think a lot of us do that in life. We're following a path someone else is navigating, with faith that we'll end up somewhere that we think we would want to be. I prefer to think of life like an old school map.

When I was taught to drive, I was taught to visualize the whole course to where I was going. I would go through the map and understand each turn. The great thing about that is I don't do the "Oh that's my turn!" and cut someone off to get over. I was able to plan ahead and be in the right lane so I don't scare those around me.

I make a lot of life decisions based on the destination, the trajectory, that I want. Since I believe in God, my trajectory is to be in heaven and live with my loved ones. That's my trajectory. A lot of decisions I make align with this ultimate goal. I've turned down business opportunities that I felt like were not in line with that trajectory.

I believe that I will be accountable to God for how I treat others. I believe my marriage is between me, my husband, and God, and I will be accountable for the happiness that I find and create in my marriage. It's more than just a contract to me. I look at my children and other people as all children of God, and that I am accountable for how I treat them. I define integrity by what God would think of me. If you break down my definition of integrity and my ultimate trajectory, that defines how I treat other people.

In terms of our driving analogy, here are the tools you will need as you move forward as a survivor.

Steering Wheel: Be in control of your steering wheel and choose the direction that you are going to go. Don't let someone else drive your car, just like you don't let someone else inside your head.

Engine: This is the mental, spiritual, and physical habits you have that move you forward. If you have a habit that isn't serving you, replace it and upgrade your engine. Take care of it. Don't ignore the "Check Engine" signs.

Map: This is your trajectory. Find a goal to strive for and visualize how you are going to get there. Decide now what you're going to do at an intersection. For examples of intersections, how are you going to reestablish your boundaries? What line are you going to draw? How will you react to drugs or alcohol? How are you going to perform in school?

Roadblocks: Realize that you cannot anticipate roadblocks, and that it's okay to pull over at times and reevaluate the road that you're on. It's okay to take breaks.

Fuel: Your emotions and feelings will motivate you to move. Are you driving with road rage? Or are you driving at safe, sustainable pace?

Natalee's Story

Two years ago on Valentine's Day I was in Vancouver, Washington for a basketball tournament. My family was in our hotel room when my brother's teammates all showed up to play Xbox. One of my brother's teammates had a hoverboard, so while they were playing Xbox I took it for a ride around the hotel, and then I went up to the third floor to babysit one of the teammates' siblings. I knocked on their door and no one answered, so I turned around to return to my hotel room. I missed the elevator, so I just kept going down the hall.

I was driving the hoverboard down the hall when someone in room 321 pulled me into his room and stole my innocence. I didn't scream, and I didn't fight back when I should have. When he was finished he said to me, "What happens in Vancouver, stays in Vancouver!" I grabbed my stuff and went back to my hotel room.

I wanted to tell someone, but I was afraid that the man might come after me. So I didn't tell my parents until ten days after we got home. It was eating me up inside that I had this secret, but I didn't want anyone to judge me.

It has been two years, and I can finally can talk about my story without crying or getting pissed off. So to the person who hurt me: I am not mad, I just want to know why you did that to me and want to know what was going through your head when you thought it was

okay to take a fifteen-year-old's virginity. Why give me that bad experience? You may be able to live with it, but that experience is a nightmare
that plays in my head over and over on constant repeat. I try to find the
pause button but it's nowhere to be found.

—*Natalee #metoo*

It's interesting to see that Natalee second-guesses what she "could
have done". She's looking to help out her brother's teammate, she's
on a hoverboard, she's doing all these normal teenage things. At that
moment, how could she have anticipated that a man would jump out
and have a response ready? Let's put the brakes on right there.

She could not have anticipated this. She could not have imagined
that kind of roadblock to appear suddenly on her way to Happy Town.
To imagine such a detour would be to imagine a life of fear.

In our trajectory analogy, the first step is to *take back control of that
steering wheel.* It's like you're driving down the road and another car
pulls up, reaches over and takes your wheel. Maybe some of us would
fight them off to regain control. Maybe some of us would just sit there
and go, "What is happening?" What the abuser did in creating this
roadblock does not change the long-term goal of where Natalee wants
to end up.

MTDMI and the psychopath that trespassed on Natalee's innocence had no right to take our steering wheels, but the first step is to
take it back, recognizing that another's choice doesn't diminish your
potential. Then, pull over to the side of the road and get that person
out of your car. Call the police. Stop the victimization from happening.
Then going forward, do not second-guess what you should have done
in that moment. You did not see this coming. You did not plan this.
Natalee was innocently walking by a hotel room. There is no should-
have that could have been done better.

But let's pretend that she was engaged in bad behaviors. She was
drinking, on drugs, dressed sexy. Let's say she was engaged in sexual

behavior then once it got a little too far said no, I want to stop. It is still Not. Your. Fault. To eliminate any misplaced shame you may feel, you need to understand who is accountable, understand the source of somebody's evil.

When things go bad, there is a biological need to analyze a better reaction. It's part of the fight or flight response. In the case of someone trespassing on the innocent, it is 100% the trespasser's fault. No matter what the victim did.

The second step is to not give him the power in part of your healing. Don't wait for him to say, "You're right, I shouldn't have done that." Once someone trespasses, that person should be removed from having any influence in your head. We have to get back behind the steering wheel, and drive to the destination that we choose.

A lot of people, including myself, do not get the reward of having the trespasser understand what he did wrong. Sadly, many victims don't even get the opportunity of having other people believe them. I'm glad that Natalee's family believed her, but Natalee is not going to get a beautiful little resolution of seeing her perpetrator in jail.

Mental health is like any other part of our well-being. Often, the body's natural impulse is to do something that feels good in the moment but will have negative repercussions if you continually do it. I like to eat chocolate. But if I eat chocolate all day, every day, bad things would happen to my body. If something happened to our mental well-being, the impulses drive us to do something that will make us happy in that moment, like eat chocolate or use drugs. Or if we go back to our driving analogy, run him over with our car. Easy emotions are anger, hate, and jealousy. They are quick and easy to have but they are hard to live with. Creating emotions like happiness, peace, and contentment are hard to make but easy to live with and are sustainable.

To create positive emotions, you must first believe it's possible and then create the habits that will bring what you want to feel closer. Happiness doesn't just come knock on your door; you have to go out and make it. But when our mental well-being is cracked open like that, if we step over the crack, those fissures will get wider and wider. Things that are important to us will fall into the crack and it's going to get bigger.

Unfortunately, even though we didn't cause this crack, we're the ones that need to build a bridge over it. Is it fair? No. *Should* we be responsible for it? No. But we have to be, because we're the ones that have to live with ourselves. We've tried skimming over it in our society, and that's what led us to this place of hurt, anger, and betrayal, with a whole lot of victims and survivors in the wake.

When I look at Natalee, who was willing to bring this forward, who was willing to make this public, who has her entire life ahead of her, I am proud of her. She understands that she needs to be the one holding that steering wheel.

The tools? Not letting someone take you off your destination. Are you going to need to pull over, gear down and wait a little bit? Yes. You'll need to stop and find resources, get professional help, learn new tools. When you're fifteen, or even forty, you may not have the tools to deal with this because it is so evil. But you need to find the power that is within us, that is divinely given, to take back control.

You can't ask other people to drive your car. There are plenty of people that are like, "Hey, um, I have a car…but I can't drive it. Will you, will you, um, will you fix it for me?" You have to fix your own car. You have to drive your own car. I know it feels almost heartless to say, "It's 100% the trespasser's fault, but you have to take responsibility for moving forward." But, if you wait for the trespasser, you're asking a sociopath to take control of your healing.

When we're driving, there are times when we may need to shift down a gear to get up a steeply inclined road. As soon as you put forward that trajectory in your mind, like getting an education, is when you are on the path to healing. We all want the journey to be easier, we all want it to go faster, but building mental resilience is not easy. It takes practice minute-by-minute, hour-by-hour, day-by-day, week-by-week, and month-by-month.

The reason the sexual abuse does not affect my every waking moment is because I started making choices that put me on my trajectory, which I didn't have fully formed for several years. However, I knew that where I was, was not a destination. This is why abuse of young people is so insidious, because the young don't understand where their life could go. It's okay if you don't have a trajectory right now. What you must do is take back your own mind, your own thoughts by being proactive about what you think about.

We can never undo the past, but we can learn from it. Our brains want to do this analysis where we wonder what we could have done better. Stop asking the question of what you should have done. Point that energy into building your future. We can't drive forward while looking into the rear view mirror.

Understand that no one takes a straight path. There are more pitfalls and valleys than grand vistas and views. In a way, that makes life easier. I think one good thing that has come from having life so hard when I was younger, is that today's simple pleasures and small moments are what make life so sweet to me. We mistakenly think there's a "destination" where we will finally be happy. I do think we'll be happy in heaven. But, along this road of life, there are still joys to be had in the journey, even if we're driving a beat-up Pinto.

And let's not judge each other for our Pintos or Mercedes. Truly we only see what other people project about themselves. We don't really know the baggage in the trunk or what kind of engine is under the hood. But if you're driving down the road looking at the other drivers, you're going to veer out of your lane or off the road or you will hit something. Keep your eye on your road, envision the map (your trajectory) and follow the direction that leads you to that trajectory. The clearer you can decide on where you're going to turn, what you're going to do at an intersection, the clearer that you will be able to access your inner power. Your perpetrator did not take *any* of your power. It feels that way, but your power is always within you, you just need to let it grow.

Emotions and feelings come. They are unique and individual, you can't just stop feeling something. You have to guide it where you want to go. For good or bad, we have thoughts and feelings. We have to fuel the ones that move us forward. *It is to God that I give the darkest emotions, and the justice system that I give evidence.* Once you can see the road ahead, you have to keep going at a pace that is sustainable. You can choose where you are going, but not so fast that you careen out of control and into other cars. There is nothing wrong with being in the slow lane with your hazard lights on, as long as you are determined to get up to the minimum speed of the road.

We all know people who expect others to push them along and then get upset their bumper is scratched. Personal responsibility is key to healing. This is not taking ownership of the assault but taking ownership of what you are feeling and processing your feelings in ways that keep you pointed toward your destination. Simply put, it will be hard, really, really hard. Get the skills you need from studying, mental health professionals, God, and from resources like this book that can guide you forward. Then go forward.

Chapter 11

Finding the Drive to Move

"I forgave him. I didn't excuse him, I just let the burden go. The burden of protecting his reputation in the community. The burden of a life trying to make people happy, so they would love me and not hurt me." –Ashley Nance #metoo

IT'S DIFFICULT TO EXPLAIN THE process of going forward because it's a moment-by-moment thing. Once you get good at the moment-by-moment, then it becomes hour-by-hour, then day-by-day, and so on. There's not just a "done." It's keeping your eye on the road. Of course we get tired, and we have to take naps and pull over at rest stops, but we need to stay focused on the road.

Truth, hope, and healing means you know who causes the pain or tiredness.

When someone hijacks your vehicle, you must stop to assess your options. We can't push our mental engine to the breaking point. The first step is to get the hijacker out of our vehicle. But, moving forward, we can't decide to never get back on the road, or to sit there as a reinforced tank. Eventually, we have to interact. Life will not let you stay in one place; it will force you to go forward. You can decide to let the traffic take you wherever, but if you put that destination in mind, you'll have to change lanes to get to the final destination that you want.

That initial decision to pull back onto the road is hard, and it's ugly. We don't like to look at ugly things. We have to find a way to be still when all this turmoil, anger, hate, and evil is taking us over. We have to be still enough to recognize who caused what, so we can then recognize what our part is to facilitate driving forward and onward. Accountability? That's his part. Shame? That comes from Satan, so we have no need for it. If you don't pick up the accountability, then you shouldn't pick up the shame. Having any of these packages in the trunk just drags on our gas mileage and slows us down.

When you look at all cultures and how they learn to be still, or however it is that you define God (yin and yang, light source, higher power), you need to be able to understand the forces of good and evil, and that every battle that has ever been fought has been between those two. We spend most of our lives living in the gray. When evil hits you like that, you have to know the good, because now you know the evil. You have to reach for the light, because now you're in the darkness. You have to reach out to your higher power to lift you up, because there is so much wanting to bring you down.

I believe that God reaches out to each of us and meets us in our Truth. He will give us that reassurance that we're on the right road. You can call it energy, but I call it the Spirit. I believe that God's light shines everywhere, like the sun, it's still shining even if we turn our back. Even if the earth turns its back on it. The night is a result of the entire earth rotating against the sun, but the sun is still shining. The moon reflects the light of the shining sun, so that even in the darkness there is still some light. The sun is always shining.

This is usually the part where people dig their heels in and say, "You don't understand *my* unique situation." It is a basic human need to be understood. Yet, why would we give the power of us moving forward to someone understanding us? Yes, the victim should be believed when he comes forward. Yes, the survivor should be validated. All of these perfect things should happen, but they're not going to in every situation. You know the truth. Don't let others drive your vehicle, particularly not an abuser. Don't let anyone else in your head.

When basic human understanding is not being given to you, that's when you put up a boundary. I like when you drive down the freeway and occasionally there are those big walls that are meant to block out the sound. I imagine putting those up between you and those who can't show basic human kindness. They still get to drive where they are going to drive, but they can't see you, and they aren't in charge of your vehicle, your happiness. Sometimes I also put up what I call my plastic shield, where I can smile and wave from behind it. Depending on their level of toxicity, I install the plastic shield or the freeway barrier.

The road has hazards and blind spots

It's a bitter truth that carjackings exist. We have seen it in the movies. People are innocently driving, then thugs with guns take their car, even point a gun at the back of their head telling them where to drive. A carjacking is really something you can't see coming, however, shouldn't we buckle up, obey the rules of the road, and look out for possibly dangerous situations? Shouldn't we look out for even innocently hazardous things, like a kid playing with a ball in the street?

We can't drive through life with our eyes watching our phones for entertainment and think everything we pass is okay. We can cause evil to find an access road when we are not keeping our eyes open for possible threats to our safety. We shouldn't drive in fear, but we do need a basic awareness. Naïveté is no defense, but we can still cling to innocence. We must be aware. How much bad happens in our world because we are not willing to see? How much innocence is lost because we just didn't want to imagine that for every incident there is a person involved? It's like when we drive by an accident and think, "Oh they must have been driving recklessly." Or do we take that as a reminder that it could have been us in that car pileup?

When in a storm or bad lighting, look to the lights of the car in front of you for assurance that you're going the right way. We need each other; we depend on each other. It is easy for us to look back into history and ask why didn't people do more to stop the evil? It's because they didn't see it, they didn't want to see it, or they were afraid.

There are few topics that most everyone will agree on. One such topic is that consent should be required for sexual innuendo, sexual words, and sexual acts. This is a rule of the road of life that almost all can agree on, and when we see someone breaking this rule, we shouldn't hesitate to call the police and, when needed, ram the perpetrator's car off the road. And yes, I mean that visual picture. Harsh. Well evil is evil, and I am not afraid to say enough. I once was, but not now.

We all want to be happy. We all want to be safe, and though we may define "safe" differently, it is our right as individuals to choose safety, but never ever to impose upon another person. I am a parent, but I give my kids choices. I give them consequences for good and for bad, but I don't get to impose, require or censor how they feel about what they view as good or bad. Only you can make yourself happy. Others enhance your happiness, but it is up to us to make it. I believe happiness, confidence, and peace all come from living in line with our ultimate destination or trajectory. Regardless of the obstacles in the road of life, we can find peace in our journey.

When we are doing what we know is going to get us where we eventually want to be, we can be happy in hard circumstances. At times we spin our wheels, but at least we are trying. If our vehicle is pointed in the right direction, we can laugh as the mud flings up and muddies the car. Or we can curse. It's all up to us. We make or destroy our own happiness.

There are lessons in everything. As a wife, I was working to put my hubby through school when we were surprised and thrilled to find out that, after five miscarriages, our first child would come in just four and half months. I had lost pregnancies as late as four months. Remember my genetic mutation? That led to difficulties carrying a child full term. As all new parents are, we were worried about money. I decided to take house-cleaning jobs so that our income was not solely from my still-growing makeup business. Time was limited and pregnancy was hard for me. One house I cleaned had nine bathrooms!

As I was cleaning a toilet, efficiency in mind, I slid into a tip MTDMI had taught me when he was grooming me to be his wife. I stopped mid-cleaning, hand leaning over the toilet, and asked myself, with emotion removed, whether this method was effective. The answer was yes, it was. I had eight more toilets, a few makeup clients that afternoon, a whole productive day ahead of me and a life, a precious miracle, growing inside of me. Was my righteous pride against this man worth not cleaning this toilet in the most effective way possible? Was I going to sloth through this to push back against a trespasser? There, in that luxurious, historic home I made the decision to own that method as one I'd gleaned from a poopy source but was a good way to clean poop. We all can sanitize our perceptions, so ask yourself not out of reflex, but out of analytical assessment with emotions removed.

There is the kind of learning we do from school, books that when pursued will get a degree from a college or university. The school of Hard Knocks awards its degree not on paper but through a million little lessons that add up to wisdom. Not all of those lessons come nicely wrapped to make us feel comfortable—they're hard. Hard lessons. Learning from them makes them have a higher purpose and sometimes discovering that lesson under all the pain helps to unravel its strength over you. You're in charge of your trajectory.

Chapter 12

Two Sides of the Same Coin

"A place for everything, and everything in its place."
– Isabella Beeton

AFTER MY MISSION WHERE I learned ASL, I returned to college to earn a degree in Sign Language. As I was in class one day, a weird topic came up and it came out that I was a virgin. I was teased quite a bit about it, which was fine. I understand that a twenty-four-year-old virgin is quite an anomaly.

There was a friend of mine in the program that was the dictionary definition of beautiful. She had the "it" factor that drives guys wild. Physically, she was the ideal, and even the way she moved was flawless. She had a string of boyfriends that she called "bed buddies." Most conversations with her revolved around sexual prowess, sexual desirability, and really, all things sex. She dressed sexy because she was sexy. I'll admit, sometimes I thought it would be awesome to have all these good-looking men adore you. She made it look like fun.

When I later got engaged to my husband, I had to give up a very prestigious spot in my program that I had worked so hard to get. My husband was in the military, so the location wasn't up to me. People were surprised that I would make that life adjustment *just* to get married.

This girl asked to talk to me after class and then pulled me around a corner. The first thing she said was, "Sex isn't that great." Well, that was a huge disappointment. I mean she was the authority on this subject.

Then something hit me and I asked her, "How old were you the first time?"

"Twelve."

"Well, we have something in common, don't we?" I told her. "We are two sides of the same coin."

After talking a little further, I learned that she had been over-sexualized as a child to the point where she felt like she had to define her worth by her sexuality. I don't know what her early sexual experiences were other than what she told me.

If women are not psychologically into it, sex is not a pleasurable experience. As one obstetrician told me, the greatest sex organ is between our ears. If the brain is excited, then all the chemistry works.

How could you be psychologically prepared for that at twelve?

"He probably wasn't very kind…"

"Yeah, he basically raped me," she said very nonchalantly. I got the idea that rape was just something that happens all the time in her world. She left me with one last bit of wisdom. "Sex is about power. It's about control."

We were like two sides of the same coin. We'd had similar first experiences with sex way too young. Both of us became very controlling. Mine was I controlled who was allowed to touch me and who was not. She became that she was always going to be the one to hold the power.

In that little alcove, I shared with her that my husband-to-be was also a virgin. "Because he could wait this long, I think he will be willing to wait until I am mentally with him."

Skeptically she said, "That *sounds* great. Will you write me and let me know?"

I agreed that I would, without giving any private information. After the honeymoon, I wrote to tell her that my experience was beautiful and amazing. All she wrote back was, "It's too late for me."

That was the last we communicated, and I don't know how her life turned out. But it pains me to think of a little girl that had something horrible done to her, and from that moment her life became a domino effect. She reacted and she responded until she was making choices she didn't fully understand. But she is still a daughter of God. She still has an opportunity to choose another way and have her self-worth fully intact.

Because we're children of God, we have the capacity for greater understanding than what we have here. When we live in a reactive state, we're empowering these negative experiences that happened to us. Even if we say that it's "what we're choosing," we're making choices based on something that we haven't healed from yet. Something that isn't serving, or empowering, or helping us. Like my friend, "It's too late for me," or, "Well I've made my bed, now I have to sleep here," or "I chose this." Where do those feelings come from that tell us we are stuck, that we can't improve, that we are powerless? Well, Satan tells lots of lies, but those are his favorite. There have been times in my life when I have been powerless, but that is not a constant condition.

How many stories are out there of people who have had terrible experiences and made it better? We can look at them and shame ourselves, or we can look at them and realize that we have capacity for greater things than what we are in this moment. But it takes diving into the concept of responsibility and accountability. We are only accountable for ourselves.

Tool #8: Organize your mental pantry

One of my favorite coping tools to use is my mental pantry. I imagine that I have a room, and in this room is everything that has ever happened to me, each experience, each memory good and bad.

Lined with shelves, this pantry stores all my life memories, hopes, failures, doubts, pains, hurts, successes, and deepest joys. I get to choose how often I access each element and what I want within arm's reach. A sign of an unorganized pantry is that you haven't chosen where things belong. You have to put each thing on the shelf you want. You will walk into this pantry often. You should decide where things go, not anyone else. I recommend putting the most useful things at easy access. If you ask an abuser to recognize what he has done and put the box on the shelf for you, then you're giving away your power.

I've come to accept that, in my room, everything is there to teach me something. On one shelf, I have Grandma Winnie, a lady who was not my real grandma but filled that role for me. The object that I associate with her is a yellow turtle that she would take and powder herself with. I also think of her floppy magazines that she would play on her recorder, because she couldn't read them, as she was legally blind. This is imagery that I have attached to her.

For MTDMI, I have a red, flashy car attached to him. It's taken awhile so that not all red, flashy cars are triggers for me.

All these different objects, feelings, and memories are in this room. Sometimes I go in and I just touch them. It's like when you're looking through a scrapbook and remembering a vacation. "Oh, wasn't that awesome? Wasn't that so funny?"

Not everything in this room is an object. Some of them are the feelings of that memory, like when my children were two and so adorable. They're never going to be two again, which I think is very rude. I like them now, too, it's just mean that they're getting so big. Some of these memories are pushed to the back of a shelf, so dusty that I don't remember them. It doesn't mean these were bad experiences, just some things that happened when I was three that I don't remember anymore. Sad I can't remember those and yet I can remember moments with MTDMI in such detail.

Our brains hold onto trauma much better than it holds onto the joys of childhood. I can remember the colors and decor of rooms and the texture of things that were around me during the abuse that happened to me.

Writing this book has definitely taken things off those shelves that I hadn't thought of in a long time. The abuse of my childhood is not one of those things that's dusty in a back corner. I remember the abuse very clearly, but I don't pick it up regularly anymore. The abuse is something that is on a shelf, where it belongs. It has molded me and affected who I am, just like the good things have. Some of those good memories can become tainted if they're associated with a person who has later hurt you.

If you take these memories off a shelf and dust them off understand that they molded you and are meant to teach you something. We don't get to just acknowledge that abuse or trauma happened and then throw them away. The abuse and trauma are now in your room. They have changed you. But when you walk into your room, is it right at eye level? Do you see it every time? Or is it up high on a shelf, where you have to reach for it?

I like to keep my pantry clean, as it's how I see if it's organized the way I want. All the bad stuff I like to put up high, so that when I'm reaching for it, I'm also looking toward God. Whenever these memories come up in a bad place or time that doesn't serve me, I can say, "No, I gave that box to you. It needs to stay up on that shelf."

In *The Hiding Place*, Corrie ten Boom's father is a watchmaker. In one scene, Corrie and her father are on a train ride to get more watch parts and she's asking him about something she heard on the playground. Instead of answering her question, Corrie's father asks if she will pick up his bag, to which she agrees.

> *"Will you carry it off the train, Corrie?" he said. I stood up and tugged at it. It was crammed with the watches and*

spare parts he had purchased that morning. "It's too heavy,"
I said. "Yes," he said. "And it would be a pretty poor father
who would ask his little girl to carry such a load. It's the
same way, Corrie, with knowledge. Some knowledge is too
heavy for children. When you are older and stronger you
can bear it. For now you must trust me to carry it for you."[8]

You have to define what it is you're asking someone you trust to carry for you. You have to label what the emotions are, where the pain stemmed from, and all the good and bad feelings that are in that box.

That box of abuse on the shelf is still mine, but I have given it to Christ. When we give something to the Savior we are saying, "You get to have that." It does not take away that it happened. It does not take away the lesson. But whenever it comes to me in a negative way, I can say, "I gave that to Christ." I can take it back at any time, whenever I decide to. I can slip back into that anger, shame, and guilt. Christ did not take it from me and hide it somewhere to be erased and forgotten. That would be nice. However, there's so much wisdom and strength that would be lost.

In my pantry full of experiences, I keep the happy memories at eye level. Whenever I walk into the pantry, all the good things are the easiest things to see. We enter alone, most of the time it happens as we're falling asleep at night. If something negative is at eye level it will inhibit us from living joyfully. To live a life free from our pain, we have to deal with it, then move that memory to a more appropriate place in the panty. Just like you have to go through the cycle of grief, through the victim and survivor stages, you have to take this unpleasant thing, look at it, and make sure you understand it. Look at all the different angles, see it in a new light, and pull out the lessons.

You may think that only the person who made a particular mistake can learn from that mistake.

----

8   Corrie ten Boom, *The Hiding Place* (Netherlands: Chosen Books, 1971), 27

As a newlywed and an army wife I was volunteering with other army wives for an upcoming activity. I was drawn to "Susan," she was fun, vivacious and always had a funny thing to say about her marriage. We all laughed. She was really funny. My friend Cynthia quietly continued her work, she didn't laugh. Her quietness struck me so I asked her about it. She simply said, "Be known as a kind wife. Then when your husband hears what you say about him he will feel your kindness." It struck me as a truth. As the next few years passed, Susan's marriage unraveled as she found someone else, then that relationship also ended. Susan's sense of humor of knocking down the man she was with didn't change. I began to find jokes that tear down spouses not as funny.

In order to pull out lessons from an experience, you need to define what is good and what is evil. For me, I label it as from Satan and from God. For some, it is defined as how other people are affected.

I do believe in God, so I have to write from the deepest, core belief that I have. I would not be authentic if I didn't speak from this belief. So when people say, "Call it God or the Oak Tree or whatever you want to call it," I'm confused, because you can't think of your higher power as just a whatever. What we call things is important. How we refer to ourselves, with each other, or with God is important. He's helped me. He's protected me. He is my friend. It's so clear to me who He is. I may not have seen His face, but I have felt His touch. My darkest moments are worth it to me, because it is so clear to me who He is. Because God is clear in my mind, I can give Him things. I say, "This is too heavy. I've opened it up. I've looked at the pieces. I understand it. I'm just going to keep the lesson, this small part that will help me fight for others. But the ugly feelings of anger and depression, I've walked through those, and I understand that I could stay there forever. But I want to be happy, so I'm giving this box to you."

Anything that we don't deal with will come back. Even things we have dealt with may come back. When disorder comes to my carefully organized pantry and these boxes topple from their chosen place, then there they are in front of me. I can look at them and say, "Oh no, I know what that is." Then I can put them back up on the shelf, because I've already given it to Christ. The more you can understand exactly what you are giving Christ, the more it becomes a habit. The more you can trust Christ as a friend to hold it.

Because those boxes from MTDMI are still in my pantry, when I hear of someone being raped or assaulted, it's like my room has been hit by an earthquake and I have to go and hold those boxes up on their shelves. Hearing others' stories still affects me. It hurts me to think of people in sex slavery throughout the world today—despite all the advances and comfort of our current society—and realize that our culture has not progressed above the need to sexually assault the innocent. I don't understand how people can become so engrossed in their own selfishness to not understand what that does to another human soul.

In time, that debilitating pain can dissipate. But if you don't trust Christ to hold it, then it will keep coming back. When I hear people don't believe in God, I grieve, because I know they have to hold those boxes, all those painful experiences themselves.

Christ walked the desert and fasted for forty days, then was tempted by Satan. Sometimes I think that we have to go through our hard times, and then look Satan in the eye and say, "I don't believe you more than I believe Him." I think we need to go back to that concept of understanding between good and evil. I have not described in gory detail what happened to me because that is looking into the eyes of Satan. I can remember it. I have dealt with it. But that is not the story and that is not the lesson that needs to be shared. In fact, in all of these years that I have talked to different survivors, it's in the victim stage that we feel the need to give a police report to our friends. Remember, you can still be a victim even if the abuse has ended. It is important, however, to give the police report to the police. In the survivor stage, we start analyzing the experience. In the advocate stage we can start teaching those lessons.

I was horrified when a neighborhood girl reached out to me recently and shared her memories of that time the sexual abuse was happening to me. Apparently, I had shared some of what was happening to me with her. I hadn't told her a lot, but I'd said too much, and it had really scared her as a child. I apologized. I shouldn't have been talking to her, I should have been talking to an adult, and I robbed her of some of her innocence. In the victim stage I told another kid, who also did not have the needed coping skills to deal with that situation.

The thing that kept me in the victim stage is the belief that my experience was somehow unique, that I was alone in my trials. Although it is uniquely individual, holding onto pain as an excuse as to why you can't do something is a really good sign that you are still in a victim stage and are looking at that bad experience every day. But worse, you have placed it in front of other happy things on your shelves and pushed all the joy in your life to the back. Reorganize your pantry to better serve you.

It takes time. When we put memories of abuse on a shelf properly, we are able to move into being an advocate. Advocates seek to use their experiences to help others, to shorten the process of recovery; they don't give victims an excuse, they give hope of what good will be in life. They cheerlead the survivor and they welcome and lift up others.

Chapter 13

The Power of Advocacy

"We find that we have become strong, capable, unstoppable and further down the road, able to reach out to help and be a STRONG voice for others!" –Gina Hamilton #metoo

I AM NOW IN WHAT I call the third phase, and that is why I'm writing this book. I'm writing this for the boy who is still in the pit at the bottom of the mountain on the road to Happy Town. I understand how you feel. I'm writing this to the woman who has chosen to push her feelings, experiences to the side and thinks that "it's too late for me." I also understand that confusion, and I'm sorry that you have to carry all the hurt yourself. I'm writing this because victims and survivors deserve to know that there is a place called Happy Town, and we can get there by the skills that we choose to develop. We can choose to be in a better place.

I call this third phase being an advocate. I am an advocate for victims of sexual abuse. Because of my experience, I have insight, empathy, and a determination to make this world better. Because of what I've been through, I have been able to protect others, in addition to my own children. This does not release the responsibility of abusers from the harm done to those of us who choose to move forward well.

My recovery is not about MTDMI. It's about me; it's about my children and my husband. It's about the imprint that I am going to leave on this world. I am still a work in progress, but I want every victim—every girl, woman, man, or boy—to know that anger is not the answer. Anger is not a destination. When we take that evil that is eating at our very souls and turn that into a backlash against society, then we are going to tear down human relations. Using anger as an approach to grief is a downward cycle that rewards Satan's evil with more evil. Satan would have abused victims become the next abusers.

You cannot tear down anyone in order to build yourself up. You can't take power from something, because then it isn't power, it's dominion. Power comes from within you. I have power over how I'm going to shape my world every morning—and I am not a morning person. This power is harnessed through the thousands of small decisions I make every day, which can bring happiness to myself and to those I influence.

I've had some very dark days, where I woke up in the morning and didn't know if I had the strength to move forward anymore. But in my dark times, I recognized that my God has always been there holding my pain. For those that don't have that, I'm sorry if this sounds trite to you, or if it sounds like sunshine and unicorns from a crazy lady. But I cannot deny the help God has given me. I'm happy. I have a good life. I like my life.

Through the goodness of God, I have been able to move into the stage of advocacy.

A dictionary definition of advocate includes:

ad·vo·cate

ˈadvəkət

1. one who pleads the cause of another
synonyms: support, uphold, back, champion[9]

---

9   Meriam-Webster Dictionary, s.v. "Advocate," accessed July 2018, https://www.merriam-webster.com/dictionary/advocate

I believe that when we deny that something happened, that is suppression. We're never really moving through the stages of grief, so we're lying to ourselves, therefore this raw emotion will pulse through us and manifest itself at inopportune times. And it will manifest itself. But once you ended the victimization, you became a survivor that dragged yourself out of the abuse. You clearly identified it was the abuser's fault, that she is accountable for the abuse, but you labeled the things for which you are now responsible. You put the shame and guilt into a box that is high on a shelf, and you have moved through the denial, anger, depression, bargaining, and acceptance. Now you are ready to become an advocate. That doesn't mean that you're perfect, it just means that you have reached a peace or clarity with reference to your abuse that allows you to stand as a pillar of strength for someone else.

Those who have experienced sexual abuse can never look upon sexual assault casually. You can move to protect others because you've been there. You can raise awareness.

The kind of advocacy that I suggest is to show the good. Show the world the good life you can lead. You can be a light for how good life can be. I can tell you the names of many women who sat me down and started conversations with me, saying, "I just had a feeling..." They were women who themselves had survived assault, and they showed me that there was hope in my future.

Many years ago, I was a Boy Scout Webelos leader for our neighborhood, and a father came over with his two boys that were around the same age as my son, and with a daughter who was a little bit younger than my daughter. We will call this girl Jamie, even though that isn't her real name. The dad was a widower, which he let me know right away. This isn't always the case, but often when someone tries to elicit your sympathy early on in a relationship, it means that they are trying to manipulate you. But at the same time, if you're a widower and moving into a neighborhood, you'll probably need to let people around you know so they can help with your kids.

This family's situation was very sad. The dad didn't work because
he had a severe alcohol addiction. So when the boys came over for
Webelos, I told the dad that the daughter could come over and play as
well. After about two meetings, I started noticing that the boys were
hoarding food. The kids were dirty and unkempt, which are signs of
neglect. But something really interesting was the way I saw Jamie hug.
It reminded me of the way MTDMI would have me hug him, something I'd forgotten. Normally a child hugs with their arms, but this girl
would thrust in her pelvis. It hit me that MTDMI would push in my
bum so that I'd give a full-frontal hug. I remember hugging a different
man that way when I was probably around twelve and he was really
uncomfortable with it. In hindsight, I learned that wasn't a normal way
to show affection. When that little girl hugged me like that, it tripped
a sensor that brought up a red flag.

Other times, I walked into the room and saw Jamie playing with a
toy and touching herself. Second red flag. I told Jamie that it was okay
for her to touch her body, and that it probably felt relaxing. I told her
we only needed to touch those parts when we need to clean ourselves,
and we clean ourselves in privacy of a bathroom. This was the way I
talked to a kindergartner about her body.

Now that I was looking for red flags, I began to notice more. There
were some severe developmental delays, which I didn't feel like had
anything to do with intelligence, but instead with people working with
her. Another thing I noticed is the way she made simple requests. My
children would ask, "Can I have candy?" They knew I would either
say yes or no. But Jamie and her brothers would hint at what they
wanted. That told me there was not only neglect, but also a fear of
retaliation. For abused children, there are consequences if the kids ask
for any kind of demand, so they learn to not ask directly to avoid direct
consequences.

I took the boys to my pantry and said they didn't have to steal
food from me anymore, all they have to do is ask and I will give them

food. They started coming over every day, and I began recording all these weird things I noticed. These children spent a lot of time in my home, and I was on the front lines of helping the dad get into rehabilitation for his alcohol addiction.

My radar was up, and I did call the police on the dad a few times when he would get into a drunken stupor. The safety of these children concerned me.

One day I was getting ready for my daughter Ailsa's birthday party and Jamie came in and asked what I was doing. I told her that I was decorating for the birthday party. My daughter had chosen a reptile theme, which she still refers to as her favorite party. Jamie told me that she had never had a birthday party before. That made me sad. "This year," I said, "you're going to have a birthday party."

I sat down with Jamie when it was her birthday and she chose to have a ladybug party. The invitations had little wings that lifted up and we released a bunch of ladybugs at the party. I ordered a ladybug cake and made little antennae that the kids would wear. It was going to be totally awesome.

I went to go pick up the cake, and to my surprise, the baker who had made it came up front to talk with me.

"Tell me about this cake," she said.

"It's for a very special young girl that loves ladybugs. Her name is Jamie."

"Where is her mother?" she asked.

I told her that she had passed away.

A little teary, the woman said, "Her mom was making the cake with me."

Whoa, right? So, we held hands and cried. I told this lady how much I love these kids, and that I'd had feelings of my own that their mother was with me. I felt like since my daughter was in heaven, that I'd take care of her kids down here if she could take care of Katelynn up there (not that she needed it, because I know Katelynn hangs out with some really awesome people). I just felt a connection with Jamie's mother.

I went from there to grab the gift for Jamie that Ailsa had thought she would want, when suddenly I stop in front of a knock-off of the American Girl Doll. Evidently, I was buying Jamie a doll. Of course, you can't just get the doll, you need to get the clothes and all the adorable things that go with it. After walking out of the store, I called my husband. That's a fun conversation I think every married couple knows.

"I just completely blew the budget."

"Oh?" He was so calm about it.

"Jamie's mom wanted me to buy her a doll." And I really had felt like there was an angel there directing me as to what to buy.

"Okay, that's great. I'm glad you followed the feeling." I have a wonderful husband.

As Jamie was unwrapping her gift, she said, "I've never had a doll before." What little girl has never had a doll? And I had noticed that when she was over here she *loooved* the dolls. I know that not every girl is into dolls, but when she so obviously loved dolls, how had no one ever bought her one before?

The birthday party turned out to be everything epic that birthday parties should be. We played ladybug games, there were ladybug crafts, we made ladybug bracelets, everything ladybug. Pinterest probably would have turned up its nose, but for Jamie and me, it was awesome. Also, I don't judge my motherhood off of Pinterest.

One day, perhaps a year after the birthday party, Jamie didn't want to go home. I looked at her and said, "Sweetie, that's where you live. Why don't you want to go home?" She just looked down at the ground. "Sweetie, do you feel safe at home?" She shook her head. I started praying.

The dad would often call me when he was drunk, and the day after Jamie told me she didn't want to go home, he made a very disturbing comment in a drunken stupor. He was talking about how he missed his wife and said that if he had a woman like me, he wouldn't have to be with Jamie. I asked what he meant. This conversation horribly scared me, but I knew that I needed more information. So far I knew his wife was dead, he had made a pass at me, and now a creepy comment about Jamie. Not okay. But when it comes to children, we need to have the bravery to hear what an abuser is saying, because we need to have evidence. He described to me how he would touch his daughter and fondle her when he was lonely. I can still tell you where I was standing as he gave me the evidence that I needed.

Once he finished I said, "How dare you. Are you telling me you can't tell the difference between a woman's vagina and a child's vagina?" I reamed him. I was angry. Then I called the police, Jamie's grandparents, the ecclesiastical leader of my area, and I would have called the president if I'd had his number. I called everyone who would give me support. Those children never spent another night in his home. After months of custody battles, the kids ended up with family that was safe. Nearly three years passed from the time I met them until they were placed with another family. I was able to come to love them just through being a neighborhood auntie.

As the legal case was going on, the attorney for the dad called me up. He asked me a couple of questions and then said, "Basically you're just some bored housewife that has nothing better to do than torment this poor, single father because he doesn't fit your ideal of what parenting is? Are you ready for the pressure of open court? There's going to be a lot of pressure that I don't think a housewife would be capable of handling."

I took a deep breath. "Do you know how to spell my name?"

"Yeah..."

"I want to make sure you know how to spell it right so that you can type it into Google. And while you're Googling me, I want you to think about how bored I am not. I want you to realize that I will thrive in open court, and I will relish the justice for Jamie. I will not rest until he has relinquished his parental rights, or he is in jail. Either way, he is not parenting these children. When you touch your daughter's vagina and sleep with her naked, you have lost the right to be a parent." Then I hung up on him.

The phone rang again, and when I answered it, the attorney says, "Mrs. Greene, I think that we got off on the wrong foot here."

"No, no, I think we got off on exactly the foot of intimidating the witness. I've already talked to my attorney and I made notes about our conversation." Oh yeah, my attorney was my husband, but he didn't know that.

Because of my own victimization, when I met Jamie I had my radar up. I became involved in Jamie's life because I loved her, and eventually I was in a place where I was able to find out the truth. I didn't shy away from the truth because I *knew* what it felt like. I knew what it felt like to be confused, to think that was love, to not know if it was okay or not. And I knew the path that she had to take to put that into a good place in her life.

I am no longer a victim and am way past surviving; I am *thriving* in my life; therefore, I can be an advocate—a champion for someone like Jaime. You can be an advocate too when you get past surviving and start thriving. I was able to stop the horrid abuse of a young girl I love because I was not reaching out in my broken pain, I was reaching out from a place of strength. It wasn't about my pain, it was about my wisdom gained through a similar experience. I am able to teach my children and empower them. I am able to look with love into a young girl's eyes and know that something terribly wrong is happening to her. I am able to stand as a *fierce* protector.

Advocacy is about reaching up, protecting, talking for those who don't have a voice. I am an advocate because I worked on me and I worked on me hard. I took responsibility for my weaknesses and understood what I needed to do for me. And I did it for me. I work on my mental and emotional health just like I work on my physical health; actually, I work on it better than my physical health.

I worked for several years as a medical ASL interpreter. I was helping a family whose daughter said her "wawa" was hurting while they were in for a routine medical appointment. When the little girl said, "wawa," I immediately got a sick feeling and thought I knew what it meant. However, the mother said the girl had been complaining for a while that her wawa hurt, but the little girl refused to say what a wawa was.

So, being silly, I showed her my arm, and I asked her if she has an arm. I showed her my pinky and the scar there and I told her how I hurt my pinky. She laughed at this. I told her I'm so silly, but I don't know if I have a wawa. Could she please show me what her wawa was? She pointed to her vagina. Mortified, her mother immediately tried to shut down the conversation, embarrassed by the topic of vaginas, but I put a hand in her face. Then I asked, "*Why* does you wawa hurt?"

This little girl then began to explain how she had been abused. Her mother, completely devastated, confirmed that she had never talked to her daughter about the proper words to use. It's important to give our kids the proper language, and to empower them to define their own boundaries for physical touch. Even something as simple as introverts who get over stimulated by too much touch need to be able to say, "I need some space." I don't want to hug people if I'm grumpy. And I don't like to hug people that I know don't like me.

Because of my experiences, I can help other victims leave that victim stage and become a survivor. I can meet other survivors and teach them about advocacy. When children, women, or men go through this, anger is not the destination. That's not where we arrive at with an attitude of "I'm going to go fight for what's mine." The destination is to become an advocate. When we look at things with that beautiful love that I believe is from God, that is where our power comes from.

Power does not come by taking it from others. It does not come by molding yourself into something hard that can never be hurt again. It does not come from demeaning all men or a certain group of people. Any time we demean anyone else, we are showing our lack of power and a lack of self-control. We are showing that our power comes from outside of ourselves, when really the power needs to come from within us.

Being an advocate also means being an advocate for you. We cannot give to others something that we do not have to give. You can do a burst of noble actions that appear heroic, but if they come from a place to be seen or to prove you are okay, you won't be able to maintain them without becoming bitter. You are only delaying your own recovery. Be good to you. Being good to you will help you to recognize what is a healthy boundary and what is a dysfunctional boundary.

One of the best tools you can employ to help you work on you is to gather great people around you. If you are hanging out with people who whine, you will whine. If you hang out with people who can't, you will be defined by your cannots. Choose awesome people to be in your circle of intimacy, those that can love consistently, be trustworthy, and those that can be accountable for their actions. Work on you, expect those around you to be working on themselves. Notice the words you speak. None of us are ever finished. Choose friends that expect great character actions from you. I married my best friend, and he helps me be the best Leta I can be.

As an example, it took my good hubby to help me see how much I still played a role in the dysfunctional family system my grandparents set up without realizing it. As newlyweds, we were at a family gathering and after dinner, I went into the kitchen and began cleaning up, because that was my job. Nathan came with me because he is a doer, and in his family culture everyone helps clean up together. We were doing the dishes when Nathan asked, "Where is everyone else?" I was still cleaning up without a second thought, as that was my job. He challenged me to leave the kitchen and not come back in until more were doing so.

I watched a drama unfold because I had interrupted the norm. In time there was clanging dishes from family members starting to do the dishes, grumbling as they did so. I joined in doing my part. I began redefining my role in my family. I left that night feeling very blessed to be married to this wonderful man. He expected the best from me because he expects the best from himself. How valuable it has been to have this honest gauge to how I was improving. His compliments mean something because they are not given to just make me feel good, they are given to help me become my best. Likewise, he takes my feedback. Our marriage enhances us.

In writing this book, I had to get feedback that wasn't always fun to receive, yet it helped this book be better than just what I could do. The contribution of my editor, beta readers, and my husband's feedback helped me see things that I was blind to. Dysfunction thrives because no outside voice is heard. In healthy relationships, we love a person as they are but also believe in his potential, and we support him in bringing that potential forward. It is our insecurities that are threatened by growth in others.

When we really love others, we don't see them as beneath us, we expect them to be living at their best. One of my favorite quotes is that, "When we treat man as he is we make him worse than he is. When we treat him as if he already was what he potentially could be, we make him what he should be." *Johann Wolfgang von Goethe.*

Chapter 14

Tools for Hard Things

"I knew nothing about what he was trying to do. For myself, the key would have been knowledge." –Mary #metoo

THREE YEARS AFTER AILSA WAS born, I became pregnant for the last time with my daughter Katelynn. We knew during the pregnancy that there were abnormalities. After she was born she breathed on her own for two days and had two corrective heart surgeries which failed. After many prayers, she was still unable to breathe on her own. My precious, beautiful daughter was dying from a condition that was irreversible, and eventually she would die from pain. Although she had been breathing through the help of a machine for weeks, her mind was still there. She could look me in the eye, something that most infants aren't able to do for a few months.

Watching her struggle, there was a moment that I got it. I had a choice. My daughter was dying from something so horrible that no pain medication could help her, and I could only watch as that pain eventually shut her body down. Or I could choose to have the life support removed so she could have a compassionate death. That is not an easy choice for a mother to make. I saw the moment that my husband also got it; we had a choice, he looked to our daughter and then to me. With a compassion and love that will never leave my heart, we were united in our understanding.

We could witness her long, painful death, or give up a little bit of time with our daughter so that she could have a peaceful passing. Her passing was something sacred and beautiful. But that's another story for another time and, indeed, another book.

It was interesting to me that the people who judged me for my daughter's death are the same people who judged me for my sexual abuse. It made me wonder why I had kept them in my life for so long. The convenient thing is they do that silent treatment thing, where they withdraw, but for the first time, I didn't go chasing after them, craving their approval.

Allow selfish people to distance themselves—we call them selfish, or toxic or whatever, but the hard part is that we do love them. Selfishness comes from a place of judgment. God always lifts us up, shows us the path, and tells us we can do it. Satan tries to tear us down.

I was talking with a woman after my daughter died. She pulled me aside and asked to talk, and I was anxious to talk with her because I knew she had also buried a child.

"Nobody can tell you how to grieve," she said. That was helpful, because I had already experienced people trying to tell me not to grieve since my daughter was born. Or I had other people blame me for getting pregnant in the first place. You know, really helpful advice like that.

"I knew the moment people had stopped praying for me," she said. When she said it, I felt a chill run down my spine, because I could see the anger and the depression in her eyes. This sinking feeling hit me that this raw emotion, this grief that I felt, was never going to improve.

I had two cousins, Richard and Dale, who died too young. I got to see how the family dealt with this tragedy. Richard was tragically run over. Dale had died in a house fire trying to save others. They could talk about the funny, quirky things they had done. It wasn't taboo to talk about them, which helped keep the essence and goodness of my cousins close. It was easy to envision them in heaven, doing good things.

Years later, Dale's sister Michele had to bury a child. So she not only dealt with burying a sibling, but now a child, and gained that empathy of what her mother had gone through. My cousin Michele was someone I felt like I could talk to, because I knew that she had gathered all the lessons from those ugly experiences and walked through the grief of it. When I buried my own child, she was a person I could look to.

When we are victims, we should have prayers. We should have support and the people who will hold us and let us cry and tell us that everything is going to be okay. But when we move out of that, we don't need to hold a press conference every day of what happened to us. People who tell their stories and say that there is nothing within their power to fix it are still in the victim stage. When you start looking at what you *can* do, what steps forward you can take, that's someone who is surviving. When those steps forward become service, giving, looking outside of just the pain of it, that's when you become an advocate.

When my daughter died, I was in a wheelchair. I had *a lot* of time to think. But I was familiar with this idea of not needing to hold a press conference every day. Do I still talk about my daughter? Absolutely. Do I hide it? No way. Is it the first thing people know about me? No. If someone asks me how many kids I have, I say three. It's the same thing with my assault. A lot of people don't know that I was sexually molested. I'm not hiding it, because I feel no shame in that event anymore. It isn't something I hide, it's just something that is high up on a shelf and doesn't need to come down unless it's appropriate or God told me to write a book. I mean, people ask you how many kids you have when you first meet them. They don't ask you if you've been molested.

In my work as a makeup artist, sitting with women and talking with them, oddly enough my experiences with sexual abuse comes up from time to time. I am able to look women in the eye and tell them that I believe God loves us and wants us to have a better life. I may cry with them. Frankly, I hope they look into my eyes and see that there is joy there, and that joy might give them hope for a better future. I say to them during one-on-one sessions that I am willing to be an example, that I am willing to show them the concept that as much as it hurts right now, and as hard as it is moment to moment, it isn't always like that.

When I saw those that had buried a child were able to still laugh it made me realize that pain wouldn't always be there, but more importantly, it made me realize that I wanted to join them.

When your focus is on the obstacles in front of you, that's all you're going to see. But when you can peek through the cracks and begin to see the vision that defines your goals, the obstacles will lessen and then fade away. Keep your eyes focused on the vision that is out there.

The gift of stepping forward carefully is that you know where you're stepping. You're able to reach out for a hand when you need one. I like to think of my Savior there, protectively watching over me, always with His hand outstretched. My guardian angels have held me up when I've stumbled.

In my youth, I spent all of my time just trying to make it through the day. I wasn't able to learn how to play the piano, or dance, or pursue my passion of art. I had not developed any talent. When I'm speaking, I often tell a story that when I was a youth in my religion, all of the young girls were asked to perform a talent. All the girls were going to do it. I sat down with my family and we all went around trying to figure out what on earth I was going to do. What was Leta good at? In hindsight it's funny, but at the time it was awful.

So my family and I thought and thought and thought about what was going to be Leta's talent. Eventually we decided. The other girls danced, played the piano, showcased their art, or played the violin. Me? I stepped up on stage with my dad and I changed a tire. Boom. Mic drop. Best talent of all time ever.

In my twenties, I recognized that my greatest talent was surviving. I may not have been racking up accomplishments at that point in time, but I was racking up character. Those character traits have served me well. As I've processed my experiences and pulled the lessons out, one of the best lessons I learned was empathy. I am not a very judgmental person because of that. I recognize that rude people may be fighting battles of which I have no concept. When a person can't give me eye contact, I don't judge why. I assume that most people are doing the very best they can. The only person I get to judge is me. Each Sunday I stop and think about my week, what went well and what didn't, how I've connected with what's most important to me, and what my shortcomings were. That's the greatest blessing that I get out of weekly church attendance. Sometimes when a trip takes my Sunday away and I haven't had that time of reflection, it is hard on me. I need it to keep me happily on track. And as the years have gone by, I like more and more who I am becoming. And I'm not done yet.

When I was confronted with falling off a psychological cliff when my daughter died, there was something that I knew this time around that I didn't know the first time I dealt with trauma. The first time I fell off that cliff, I fell all the way to the bottom, knocking me to my core. I'm surprised that I survived. I'm very proud that I figured out a way to get up, as bleeding and raw as I was.

With the conversation in our society, it becomes very easy to say, "Me, too." I remember the first time I saw that hashtag on Facebook and it was like a sucker punch because I could say yeah, that happened to me, too. But with that barrage of negative feelings, I remembered the lessons it has taught me. Then came a wave of mixed emotions.

I was grateful for those lessons when my daughter died. I transitioned from being a victim of death to a survivor of death relatively quickly, because when it came to the grief stage of anger, I knew anger. I had done bargaining. I'd had depression. I knew what it was like to fall down that cliff. So when I again felt myself falling off this cliff, I said "wait," and I looked to my God to give me wings to fly back up.

I put a vision before me. I set up my trajectory. I told myself that someday, I would be with my son, and he would be with his wife, and she would be holding their first child. Someday my daughter would be with her husband, and they would be holding their first daughter in their arms. When each of those darling babies reach fifty-four days, which is how long Katelynn lived, they will realize that I said goodbye. Then they will think back to their mental room full of happy memories, bonding and connecting with each other and with me, and they will remember me showing them how to grieve in a healthy way. They will hear my laughter. They will hear my tears. They will remember when they said, "I miss my sister," that I said, "I do, too."

Recently, my fifteen-year-old son came into my room and said, "Mom, you're a fighter." I laughed. "Why yes I am. Why do you say that?"

"I was looking at family pictures, and I came across a video of you holding Katelynn. You're a fighter Mom." He talked to me about how he felt. My son knows I'm tough, and he knows I'm a fighter. What greater gift could he give me and I him, but to be a fighter?

In order to have my daughter's death not hurt me, I would have to turn off love. I would have to turn off connection and become a hardened version of myself. The longer we stay in anger, the longer we stay in depression, then we allow the theft and grief of it all to mold us. Staying a victim is understandable. It is. You have every right to stay in the stages of anger or depression.

But I would put in front of me this vision of what I was going to become, of what my children's fleeting childhood would be. Because, yes, I could take the next ten years grieving my daughter's death, and that would be understandable. But I don't get those ten years of Nathaniel's and Ailsa's childhoods back.

It took me almost eight years to get to a good place after my sexual abuse stopped. Then I went on a humanitarian mission and realized I wasn't as whole as I believed I was, but at least I was focusing on God. When my missionary service ended, I had developed tools of trust, of peeling back the lesson, of how to assess my relationships, how to judge my relationships. Those tools helped me pick a good partner to become my husband. I was able to create healthy relationships.

Many of those lessons, and that strength to hold onto that lesson, comes from that flashy car on the shelf in my memories. I don't envision his face because it's uncomfortable to me, so that's why I have the car. I slammed his car door once, which was the first step of power that I took, my first act of crazy defiance. I can laugh at it now, because it really wasn't all that dramatic of a scene, but it was a turning point of me sticking up for me. That's how I've packaged it. The dark, ugly moments I have given to my Savior.

Back then, as a little girl, I did not understand where I wanted to go in life. In writing this book, I realize that there may be some victims who can't imagine a life full of happiness ahead of them. If you can't envision it, will you please borrow my vision? Will you please understand the vision that I have for you? It's the vision that God has for you. I don't think God causes the bad things to happen. I believe that He allows agency to play out, that He allows human beings to act, which often results in unsavory consequences for victims. But I also believe that bible verse that says, "And we know that all things work together for good to them that love God." (Romans 8:28)

I believe that He says, "Take this lesson, and I promise you that things will work out." He didn't cause this to happen to you. But God is saying, "I will promise you I will make it good." He's fulfilled that promise to me.

To a twenty-year-old girl who may not have found her forever man, be picky. You deserve to be picky. Don't give your soul and your body to someone who only sees your body. To that thirty-year-old man who may be surrounded by a few kids now but finds those dark shadows of past abuse creeping in during the night, I'm sorry that I can't tell you why that's happening, and I'm sorry I haven't had that same experience. I realize that may be a little odd, but I wish I could tell you how to deal with this.

If you've spent the bulk of your years raising your kids by cutting off your love, I believe in second, third, and fourth chances. I kept that vision of what I wanted my life to be after my daughter's death close to me, in order to honor her memory. The same coping skills I used to make it through her death are the skills I learned from surviving and then thriving through my sexual abuse. I put all that yucky stuff into the arms of someone that I trust, my Savior.

But you have to understand the nature of God. That's the first step. When people say they don't need religion, it isn't something I understand. I need that weekly accountability. I have weekly accountability in my business, in my family. Any good coach or mentor is going to give you tools that will help make things quicker for you because they give you a vision. I only gather around me those friends that are happily married. If someone is ragging on her husband, I don't keep her around me.

Every decision in my life has to fall in line with my trajectory for my life. I have to put my effort and energy into my grand vision, and thus stay in control of my destiny.

Chapter 15

Power of Hope

"Give your best anyway. In the final analysis, it is between you and God. It was never between you and them."
–Mother Teresa

WHEN IT CAME TIME TO release my daughter from this life, it wasn't even a question if I was going to check out, because by this time I had developed better coping skills. I kept collecting those skills as I hiked up the mountain and drove my car along the winding roads of life. I had become more aware of what I was or was not capable of enduring. To say you can't move forward because of a certain condition like anxiety, depression, or PTSD is like saying you can't drive your car because you have a four cylinder and wish you had an eight cylinder. The cool thing about this car analogy is that you can always upgrade your parts, but we're still driving a car.

When we say we can't do things, it's giving power in our life to the experience or abuser or to a particular condition. All of these things are brain chemistry. They are very real and very hard, but they do not limit the ability of the brain and body to do certain things. They are like a hormone that floods our bodies, and I think we can get addicted to being in a condition because it's scary to pick up the pace in life and to drive faster.

Brain chemistry is a reaction. When you are able to recognize that you are having a reaction is when you gain the ability to choose a response. You can look at the situation and realize *this is my body, this is my brain chemistry reacting like this*, but it may not be the reaction that you want.

I have PTSD, and PTSD often has very specific triggers. Seeing MTDMI would be more than a trigger, it would be like a machine gun taking me out. Hearing certain phrases can also trigger my PTSD. These triggers can be huge things like dealing with the abuser all the way down to things I have to deal with in day-to-day life, like loud, sudden or repetitive noises.

I hesitate to write a book about my weaknesses because I have people that want to hurt me. I'm speaking on a sensitive topic, so that's bound to bring up the haters. I've already experienced people attack me on social media when I wrote my #metoo post. I also have people that I love that are not capable of loving me the way that I need them to. It's hard to be like, "Oh by the way, here's the ammo you need to get an immediate chemical reaction from me."

I have jumped at loud, sudden noises and will probably always jump at them, but I can smile at that and laugh afterwards. I recognize that a hormone just flooded my brain that is processing cortisol and adrenaline, triggering my fight-or-flight instincts. I can recognize this truth and label it, and then I begin asking questions. Am I literally under attack? No. Am I in danger? No. A kid just dropped a toy. When this chemical reaction is firing off, I have to wait, gather facts, and determine what's the truth.

When I go into a situation where I know there will be loud noises, I have to prepare myself. Now keep in mind that I'm a professional speaker. There's a loud, repetitive noise that happens at the end of every speech! Isn't that ironic? There's something funny about the fact that people are thanking me and I'm sitting there thinking, "It will end soon, it will end soon, it will end soon, oh good it's over." I had someone ask once if I speak because I love the applause. Nope, not really. I remind myself what the applause means. It's a thank you from the crowd, so I've been working on looking in the audience's eyes and sending back the love. Sometimes I just have to hurry off the stage.

So the kids I have now were once babies that would cry. I know, it's hard for me to imagine, too. My daughter actually had colic. When Ailsa screamed as a baby, I would feel jittery, shaky, and my gut would be screaming at me to run. I would be over-stimulated, but I would check in on what was actually happening in that moment. Was I actually under attack? No. Then I would project what I wanted to happen. I wanted this baby to grow into a healthy toddler. Then I would focus in on the good. I would look at this sweet baby and it would ground me. But if I only focused in on the loudest noise, the screaming, and how it made me feel, then I would miss the good that was happening.

The screaming only lasted for so long, but I would have to logically walk my way through it. I would have to grab tools and work on my vehicle. I would be still when I needed to be so that I could ground myself. If at any time I was unable to walk myself through that, then I would need to go to my first recourse of action, which was to ask my husband to hold the baby because I just wasn't doing it well tonight. You have a much higher ability to get people to understand what you are saying if you say, "I am doing this to help me, but I need additional resources." It goes over better than telling someone to drive your car. Or to say that you're feeling sad and someone else is responsible to fix it. Nobody else can fix it for you. You have to be doing something, actively endeavoring to fix yourself.

Mentally I had to pick those tools up instead of just going with the flow of how I felt like responding. If at any point you realize you can't pick up those tools, don't cover up those feelings: that's where you need to get mental health professionals.

My PTSD has made me more symptomatic in choosing which of those tools I need and how often. I don't think the tools are the same for everyone, as you have to figure out what works for you. I found singing favorite gospels songs to be a great reducer of cortisol. My kids could sing these songs at a young age. Walks were great. I'd load the kids in the stroller and as my pace picked up, the cortisol levels would diminish. Exercise is a great way to de-stress.

No one can make you pick up your tools. No one can make you drive. But life will force you to react, and when you do react, which tool are you holding? Is it a hammer, or is it a knife? Is it something that will help fix you, or is it a weapon to cut down all those around you? You get to choose that reaction by checking in with what's true.

I believe that, because of my brain chemistry, I have a more finely-tuned engine for using various tools. Due to my PTSD, I have to consistently think through why I do things and what is an appropriate reaction. As a result, I better tend to the little nooks and crannies of my psyche. Because I was in a depressive state for years, where I just wanted to die and cease to exist, I hold onto the light all the more—I don't take for granted my mental health. Because I know the difference, I do not neglect the vehicle that drives me forward. I recognize when I'm having a harder time picking up my tools. I recognize that when my focus on the road is slipping, that's when I ask for help, knowing that ultimately it's on me to not only seek help, but to implement the tools I have.

I think going to therapy is an essential step to finding mental well-being. But once I have the tools, I am able to use them anytime. I don't live in a therapist's office.

When someone says they can take away my PTSD—and believe me, plenty of people have tried to sell me magic pills—I can't hear that in the way that they mean it. You're going to take all my pain away? I already have a path that helps me use that as fuel. When I feel that touch of anger or that touch of despair, I take that moment to work on myself. It fuels me to be my better self. I do not let that anger take the front seat. I let it burn up as fuel to drive me forward. I could never say with confidence, as empowered as I am, that there won't be moments where I am triggered. When I hear that someone else has been molested or abused, I hope that I never become jaded at that. Wouldn't that be losing my empathy? That seems like a pretty cold and hard existence.

I love that evil tried to mold me, and instead I became a loving person. I'm really proud of my choice of love, which ultimately has come as a result of the sexual abuse perpetrated on me, the loss of my daughter, and the other many trials, including health challenges. I know I am not alone in having trials and challenges. But, I don't let the negativity of these events take the front seat, as negativity is not fuel-efficient. I get to decide where my vehicle goes, and where those negative emotions are put in my car. So can you.

I believe that when God touches our hearts, we are called to His service. We need each other. We need to put boundaries up to those who seek to drive our vehicles off the road. Find motorists that know how to use a blinker and are capable of communicating with those around them.

When we drive down the road, we have bumper stickers on our car. I never want to be the car that says, "Has PTSD, was sexually molested, buried a kid." I want my bumper stickers to be, "Peace, Love, Chocolate, Kindness." I want to radiate love, truth, kindness, empathy, charity, and compassion. I am so proud that I have been able to find this place.

Saying that "I can't" is asking the world to moderate to your limitations. It won't. Stop asking the world to alter its pressures on you. Asking the world to stop is actually stopping you from being what you can be. It's stopping you from going to the next place where you can have joy, experiences, connections, and beautiful vistas that show you how wonderful life is.

When an alcoholic enters Alcoholics Anonymous (AA), his goal is to enter into recovery. He will always be an alcoholic, even if he no longer drinks, because alcohol is something he will always have to guard against. It would be irresponsible for an alcoholic to consider himself cured and return to his previous lifestyle or circle of friends. The last step of AA is to try to help other people. That's when we move out of this survivor mode. We have used these tools enough that we feel confident that we can help others. It's as if you've had enough experience fixing your own car, that you can slow down and help another stranded motorist change a flat tire. But, you'll be worse than useless if you don't already have a working car.

As a freshman in college, I went to my religious leader to confess all my sins. I told him what MTDMI had done to me, eager to repent of my wrongdoings.

My leader looked at me and said, "How long have you felt bad about this?"

I told him that I had talked to God but had never cleared it with Him.

"How long?" he asked again.

"Well he stopped when I was thirteen."

"So for five years you've believed that you had some blame in this?"

"…yeah."

"No. You had no blame in this. None. This was him, not you." He looked at me from across his desk and said, "You need to put this at your Savior's feet. And don't for one more moment think this was your fault."

After a moment of silence, I replied, "I guess that's all I have to say then."

I will forever be grateful that my religious leader responded that way and recognized the truth. Regardless of what I believed was the truth at that time, he recognized that I was blameless and was able to start cracking me out of the confines of the shame I had lived in for so long. My leader responded the same way that I believe Christ would have handled it, placing 100% blame on the abuser.

Once I was able to label the truth of who was at fault and could clearly define it, I could take control of what was mine. One thing I love about church is that it's a time once a week that I am still. I get to think about how my week was, where I'm going, why I'm doing it all. It really helps me see if I'm slipping in my well-being. Our world is so fast-paced that we don't pick up on the sputter in our engine unless we stop and listen. Many people drive until their engines completely break down, having ignored the check engine light

When we are stressed, our bodies do not know the difference between a bear attacking us and being stuck in traffic. The hormone reactions are the same. It's up to us to stop and say, "What's the truth? Am I under attack? Am I not?" Then breathe, meditate, pray, exercise—I know, I hate that exercise is the answer, but moving the body gets that cortisol out of there. If you are dealing with the after effects of abuse, that excess cortisol will pump through your blood and tear down your muscles, damaging your engine. You need to move your body to release that extra cortisol, get it out of your system.

To recap, here is a list of tools you need:

Tools

1. Creating the Circles of Intimacy using love, trust, and accountability
2. Recognize the stages of grief
3. Understand accountability, blame, and responsibility
4. Focus on your thoughts and words
5. Know how to forgive to be free
6. Make the hike to Happy Town
7. Pick your trajectory and drive your car
8. Organize your mental pantry

Follow the light. Get a destination that is bigger than yourself to work towards, which is called trajectory. Focus on the good and move forward and find the good in the moments. There are resources available from therapists that can arm your tool belt with what you'll need. Once you have the truth, you can know that power is in you. Within your soul, you will know when you are on the right track. Your body knows when you are on the right track. It will shut down and make you sick, unless you get on the right track. That light within us will help us to recognize the truth of what we need to look for and do. But we can't pour toxic into our bodies or souls and expect good results. We have to recognize the good and the evil, distinguish what we're dropping and then move forward with the good that we're taking along our life journey with us.

Once we're stuck in traffic and feeling that stress, we need to understand that we are not under immediate threat and reach for our tools. One that I use is repeating good things that I see around me. Some people meditate, some use listening to uplifting podcasts. Sometimes I simply change the kind of music that I'm listening to. There's a good way to do this and a fake way to do this.

The fake way is using drugs, alcohol, or other stimulants and addictions like food, TV, or our phones. If we're using something to cover up pain, chances are it's an addiction. If we're doing it from a place of, *I'm really stressed out so I'm going to focus on something that I can control,* as long as it is healthy, then it's okay to use. Putting on music that makes you want to dance is good. Going on a major shopping spree that damages your budget is not.

Pumping your body full of good endorphins by using gratitude or exercise will help you start to be able to pull apart what is true and what is not true. Once you can distinguish that, you can take a moment and breathe, maybe cry if you need to because it really hurts, and then you can judge what your next action is going to be. That way if the baby is screaming you don't just throw him out the window.

What's real, and what can I do with that? I often put myself in timeouts. In my car analogy, I always have my children as passengers, because I am molding their psyche. So I will turn to them and say,

"Mommy is really stressed out right now. I need to pull over and take a minute." There's nothing wrong with telling them you need some compassion. Children do not need to know what exactly is wrong for them to be able to have amazing, compassionate responses. I can tell them that Mommy is having a hard time right now, and she is going to go cry for five minutes, and then she is going to do something to make her feel better. Like having a dance party with my kids. That's healthy for them to see. They don't need to know what I'm crying about.

I also have a go-to song that's about Christ that's almost like a prayer to me. It's a tender thing that my kids started to pipe up and sing it with me as young as two.

When sadness hits me, I get to take a moment and ask myself, "Is my reaction what I want right now?" I have a choice of bingeing on chocolate (can't say I haven't done that one before), but that isn't teaching my children or me an appropriate response to stress. If I'm about to get on a stage, I can't take that time to deal with issues right away. I'm just not going to get up there and be angry and sad in that moment. But, at an appropriate time, I am going to deal with it and feel those emotions. I'm not going to suppress or forget what caused that stress. I dictate how much time I'm going to put into things, then I get my body chemistry going, and then I move forward. I get myself involved in an activity that is in line with my goals, my goals of heaven, my goals with my family, my goals financially. I don't stay sad. As you're moving forward, you start to feel better because you're changing up your brain chemistry.

Accordingly, the first step is I give myself an allotted time to feel everything. That amount is based on what I logically have thought through the time I will need. Then I get some movement in my body and I start focusing on something better. Then I go do something good.

To reiterate the formula: Follow the good, focus on something positive, and be honest with those in your inner circle if you need to be. All of this relates back to the trajectory.

Just because something happened to us does not mean we are forever ruined. We have been dented, hijacked, and beat up, but we are fixable. Even though my blood tells the history of what I have been through, I still have a happy life. There is hard stuff that has gone down in my life. Hard stuff. But I don't need to tell everyone that I come across here's my life story in a book. Oh wait...

When we're in the survivor phase, we have this need to go around and tell everyone what happened to us. But when we're in the advocate phase, we get to choose to share that only with those that need to hear it from us. Only with those that need it.

I am not ashamed of anything that has happened to me. I no longer let shame drive my car. God never shames us. Even when that woman is taken in adultery, he doesn't shame her. (John 8: 1-11) He tells her to get back in her car and drive. When a man approaches Christ and asks Him to heal his child, the man says, "I believe, help thou mine unbelief." (Mark 9:24) When we go through this process of truth to following the light in our path of healing and we don't feel like the light is getting in, we can ask God, "Help thou mine unbelief."

I know that God's light can touch our dark places. You and I do not have to believe the same principles to know that light is truth. We can ask Him to help our unbelief. The most horrible thing that evil does is try to block out the light.

One of the greatest lessons I have learned to finding happiness is not to ask *why me*, but to ask myself "*what am I to learn from this*?" Life isn't fair. Thinking life is fair will only make you angry and asking the questions that can never be answered. Why me? Why did she do that? Learning why another person would attack someone is not a place I want to spend time thinking about. I am thankful that there are professionals that seek to understand, yet for me that is not the key to my recovery.

Is it naive to think that one by one our declaration to become more, to be more than survivors and choose to heal could really change our world? Perhaps. But as evil finds strength in secret acts, could not the opposite also be true? When we know great evil, when we know great hurt, the contrast to the dark is light. Who better to recognize the light than those that know darkness!

It's simple, so simple that it doesn't seem possible in contrast to the immensity and breadth of sexual assault, yet my heart knows that the path to healing has come from seeking the light. Why give darkness such authority? Even if my advice is naive to the world at large, it absolutely will alter the lives of those affected.

Darkness always comes, but light comes and chases it away. Every. Single. Time.

I choose hope.

I choose it and peace has found me. I may have scars, but they show me the promises we believers know exist. Many may see that as naive— yet for thousands of years, millions have endured the unspeakable and come out crediting God. Why not take the unspeakable and shed light on it? Help those that are affected know they are not alone.

Great change starts within each of our hearts. Let's talk. Let's keep talking. Let's remove the stigmas and judgment. Let's educate our children to recognize the dangers that exist and to turn from them. In turning from dangers, they will be able to clearly see evil for what it is. In this we protect them. Words have power. We cannot suppress the words of anyone: young or old, male or female, gay or straight, religious or not religious. In sharing our hurting places with respect, we will find understanding.

Chapter 16

Parents Must Provide Safe Spaces

"I felt betrayed because during those times no one ever spoke about anything. If anyone knew about my abuse, they simply didn't want to get involved." –Yolanda #metoo

SINCE MY FATHER WAS A truck driver for a living, he often took one of us along to help him on his routes. Back then they were not family-friendly travel centers. Truck stops were greasy, grimy places, complete with prostitutes called lot-lizards and pornography readily available. At times when I was with my dad, he would dress me up as a boy—all he had to do was tuck my braid behind my collar because I wore my brothers' old clothes—and he'd hose me off in back instead of sending me into the showers alone.

I remember helping my dad run some electrical cable from the back of the mobile home to the front. I came around the corner of the truck, out of sight of my father, and a man grabbed me. He started pulling me away so quickly that my legs drug behind me as I stared down at the gravel. I could feel the evil emanating from this man.

I called out, and my father was instantly there. The man dropped me, as I am sure the sight of my father's sturdy 6'3" frame frightened him. Imagine the emotions that must have been coursing through my dad: anger, fear, and horror. But instead of acting out in his anger, my father took me up in his arms. He could have chased after that man or shouted vulgarities, but instead, he remembered me. He put me first. When I think of my childhood, that moment is one I used to define safety.

When something happens to your child, do not respond in front of them in your anger. A child in trauma has an even harder time understanding that the anger is not directed at him. Comfort her. Embrace him. Create a safe place for your child to talk and begin to sift through the accountability, blame, and responsibility. When your child is taken care of and safe, then you can pursue your justice.

As parents, we are accountable for being the best parents we can be. But at the same time, there is only so much that we can do. I know my parents feel a great sense of loss that they couldn't protect me better. But there is nothing they did that caused the sexual abuse that happened to me. The responsibility is on the trespasser. They didn't know what was happening, therefore they have no blame. MTDMI could see their flaws, including my mother's deepest hurts, and he manipulated that pain for his own purposes. He wove his way into our lives and earned their trust and then betrayed it. He violated them in a different way than he did me, but it was still an unthinkable violation.

Horrifically, there are parents that do molest their children or allow them to be molested. A young girl I knew told her dad she was being molested by a neighbor. His response was that it was okay because the neighbor didn't have any daughters of his own. I met her when she was nineteen, so she'd endured several years of abuse at the hands of her father and her neighbor. My husband and I were able to take her into our home for a couple of years. She has since married a wonderful man that honors and loves her, and with whom they have created a beautiful family. She told me that she learned what love is from watching my marriage. That is one of the best compliments that I have ever received. She decided to stop the domino effect. She didn't have a protective father. I did.

If your child has been molested and it wasn't something that you foresaw or participated in, guilt is a useless emotion. We all have weaknesses. We all have things we could do better. Shame and guilt come from Satan. Hope and a desire to do better come from God. There's a difference between Godly sorrow and ruminating. Once God has forgiven, move on.

Depending on the age of your child, you may need to advocate for your child with the police and within the justice system. There are professional organizations that help with advocacy, use every resource you can find. Don't sweep it under the rug. Don't hide what happened to your child simply to avoid awkward conversations. Children need to talk, and the best person for them to talk to is someone who loves them. Unresolved pain manifests itself in ugly ways including, but not limited to, cutting, drug use, suicide, and criminal behavior.

What is a parent to do? First, we must recognize the millions of victims each year and that abuse is happening in homes not so different than our own. According to www.DoSomething.org, 68% of victims are sexually abused by a family member, 90% know the abuser. Can I add to the horror of these statistics? These numbers come from *reported* cases. In one of my college apartments, three out of the four of us had been sexually abused. Each of us knew our abuser.

Sexually abused children are 59% more likely to be arrested as minors, 28% more likely to be arrested as an adult, and 30% more inclined to commit a violent crime than children that were not abused. They are also more inclined to practice casual sex, since those boundaries were eroded and not reestablished. Casual sex puts them are risk for sexually transmitted infections and the girls are 25% more likely to become pregnant.

We cannot walk away and tell ourselves that this is not our problem. It is our problem, it is a societal problem that is eroding our mental health. But we can change this problem. We can learn from this, we
can arm our children—those within our influence—with knowledge
at an age appropriate level. Carry the load for our children as Corrie
ten Boom's father did for her. Teach children the many little lessons
of self-awareness, boundaries, and coping skills that will aid them as
they navigate life. How do we teach them? By first learning these skills
ourselves and then talking to them.

Kaci's Story

A friend of mine who wishes to remain anonymous shared with
me her experiences with sexual assault. We will call her Kaci. Kaci was
almost date raped, but she was lucky enough to grab his keys, throw
them in the sage brush and says she "was a track star that night" running home.

Years later as a mom, Kaci noticed her daughter stopped wearing
shorts one summer, and her husband noticed bruises on her arm,
that looked like they were caused by fingers gripping her. Kaci's
daughter never told them anything. She just quit her job and stopped
hanging out with her good friends. About a year later, she came to
Kaci late one night and told the story of what almost happened and
confessed feeling unworthy of dating again. Kaci told her daughter,
"You fought back and won." Kaci addressed her daughter's feelings of
self-doubt with an affirmation that she was not a victim, she was a
fighter.

It's interesting how the same attempt was made on both mother
and daughter, and as a mother Kaci was able to take the wisdom of her
trauma and tell her daughter what she needed to hear when she was
ready to talk about it. I also think that her parents noting what was
happening with their daughter gave her a safe place to talk about her
fears and pains.

Wendy's Story

In contrast, my friend Wendy from Australia shared her story of how her mother did not create a safe space, enabling the abuse Wendy and her brother endured.

"My mother decided to marry her long-term boyfriend when I was ten years old. In the early stages of their marriage, I felt my brothers and I were denied love even though we had a roof over our heads, clothes and food. The abuse started when I was about eleven. Sexual, emotional, and spiritual abuse toward my younger brother and me, but my younger brother's abuse was much more severe than mine with traumatic bashings, neglect, and verbal abuse..

"My stepfather was my 'father figure,' I knew no different as he had control and power over me. My stepfather made comments when he knew I was having my period, and this made me feel uncomfortable because my grandparents taught me not to openly discuss matters like menstruation. I couldn't even ask my mother to purchase sanitary pads for me, I was so fearful of how she would react, so I used a lot of toilet paper. My grandmother bought my first bra.

"I have had numerous counselling sessions and I still feel somewhat affected today but, being a mature woman, I know I have become wiser and I have been influenced by others that have come and gone in my life. I am thankful to my mother for showing me the parent I did not want to be. I provide my children with love, support and valuable communication skills. We have a fabulous relationship and I am truly blessed and grateful.

"Today I am wiser, have grown mentally and spiritually, and have had no relationship with my mother for over thirty years. She has not met my husband of eighteen years, nor my two teenage children. I am in contact with my father's side of the family, and I am proud to say I am blessed and grateful, happily married with two gorgeous children."

–Wendy #metoo

There are many gory details to Wendy's story that don't need to be shared, but suffice it to say that Wendy's mother chose to aid the abuse to her children by her silence. The cost of her non-action is that she has no relationship with her children.

Parents must provide safe places for their children. Allow them space to talk to you and know that you won't explode or punish them. Most importantly, don't try to silence them for your own comfort.

Chapter 17

How to Talk to Your Kids

"I wanted to puke. I had failed my baby." –Ashley Nance #metoo

WHEN MY KIDS WERE LITTLE, I talked to them about superheroes. My oldest is a boy, so superheroes are a natural conversation. One Halloween, to his glee, he got to pick out a slick Spiderman suit. It was not uncommon after this costume acquisition to come around the corner with a basket of laundry to learn that I had suddenly been webbed! I would fall to the floor in mock anguish, restrained by webs only my son could see. He would be a little disgusted that I didn't always take the webbing blow in the right place. How could I not know where I'd been hit? It was a mystery to his young mind. We had a lot of games and talks about superheroes.

I wanted Nathaniel to see the superhero in him, knowing that, just like Spiderman and his friends, my son would have to face growing into his strengths. He, too, would have to fight battles; he, too, would have to face down evil. It has been one of my life's greatest joys that the deepest distress he faced in those days were imaginary foes lurking behind cabinets, hiding in the pantry, and terrifyingly slumped under his bed at night.

As he explored the world with childlike eyes, I knew that real danger could be out there, but it was my job to carry that threat. I let him believe that his webs would ward off any concern. I would hide behind him when informed of an oncoming threat. Of course, in real life we don't know when the threat is coming, and we may not feel prepared in the face of evil assaults. And in real life I wouldn't hide behind him.

Some evils are so ugly that our temptation may be to hide, but that is a choice that allows evil to win. Let's be very clear, as much as I would love to say that my son wouldn't have to face down evil villains in life, it isn't reality to presume I can always protect him. And if I were able to do so, when will he discover his greatness? When would he find that he can stand against life's blows? My job as a mom is to push him into the world as soon as he is able to deal with it.

Get Comfortable Talking About Sex

As parents, we want to protect our children. It's hideous to think about something terrible happening to them, but sometimes the hideousness of the threat stops our minds from creating defenses. We must have conversations about body safety even though they are uncomfortable and even though they weren't had generationally.

Think back to those fabulous *I Love Lucy* episodes that had a married couple staying in two separate beds. Hollywood has no problem now bringing those beds together, even if they aren't married. Children see this and come away understanding that to be touched is desirable, that it's part of growing up. We can't leave sexual education to the media, and we must stand ready to correct the record for our children.

For years, society said it was improper to discuss anything remotely touching on the idea of sex, but we as parents need to be comfortable talking about these things with our children in a good way. Obviously, you aren't going to walk up to a three-year-old and say, "Mommy and Daddy have sex." There are human developmental stages of what children are ready to comprehend. A friend told me that her daughter came to her and asked, "Mommy, what is sex?" She asked her why she asked. She had seen a paper present options of "Sex (circle one): M or F." Your child may not be asking what they think they are asking. Posing follow up questions will help give them the information they need and not more than they need to know for now.

If we aren't comfortable talking to our kids about this, who will? We need to be very comfortable talking to our children about their bodies all the way up to discussions about sex, because their peers are not uncomfortable talking about it. Hollywood is not uncomfortable *showing* it. What information do you want them to have? It is not a matter of if our kids will be exposed to pornography, but when. Our kids are being exposed by the time they are eleven and as soon as eight years old. They are being shown images and ideas that some of us adults may never have seen or imagined. The age of innocence that we pray our kids will have is not a timeline for which we are in control. When my kids come with questions, I answer them, discussing with them the physical, emotional, and physiological ramifications of each question. As I am religious, I also share the spiritual aspects of what they are asking. It does not place me in the situation of saying to them, "you can't do this." This allows me to present them with choices, consequences, and rewards of any action and what I suggest they do.

Help Your Children Develop Boundaries

Ignorance is not bliss. Ignorance primes our children to be targeted because they don't understand what is appropriate or not appropriate. We should not shy away from answering their questions. As age and psychologically appropriate, we need to teach them how to develop boundaries. We can teach pre-kindergarteners autonomy, that they are in charge of their own bodies, and they should only touch their private parts to clean them. When my kids were in the tub, I would assign body parts to them to clean, such as their tummy. Once they had mastered cleaning that body part, it was now their job. It wasn't anyone else's job. They were in charge. Two-year-old kids *love* this.

When it came time to potty train, I passed to them the responsibility of their private parts, and explained they are parts we don't show in public. In kid cartoon shows, when the bear mooned the other forest animals, I would say "Oh my, why is he showing one of his private parts?" I knew that the bum is an area that molestation and assault can happen, but I didn't tell my kids that. We had a discussion about private versus public, and those body parts are different because of their use. I didn't want them feeling body shame. I was setting them up for conversations we could have later about all the useful purposes of our bodies. We also explained that mommy and daddy won't be touching their bum or penis/ vagina anymore. "You're getting so big, so you are in control of your body and responsible to keep it clean." I gave our body safety talks centered on the idea that as you get bigger, you get more choices and responsibilities. Not only did my kids become in charge of their own bodies, they also became more in charge of their messes and cleaning it up.

Removing the shame around what we must do for our bodies opens up conversation. My son learned this when he peed on the neighbor's tire in front of our house. It was an opportunity for me to teach him about peeing in public. The conversation was for others' property that we don't put our pee on people's things because our pee is something our bodies don't want anymore. We don't put our trash that we don't want in others' yards either. It was almost a side note that I said we have doors on bathrooms because we pee in private. I explained there was a good reason he had never seen the neighbor man pee in his own yard. Families may do some things around each other, like peeing on a tree when camping, but we don't pee around everyone or on anyone. Yes, that last part will need to be covered, am I right moms of boys?

I taught my kids to check in with their feelings, learning to monitor themselves according to the light and darkness they could feel within.

Obviously, when they're little, their feelings may involve simple things like the contrast of feeling bad due to contention from a fight versus feeling good when they're sharing.

I also didn't require hugs for apology or affection. An apology is in your tone and attitude. Talk to me and others in a nice tone, because that's respect. If someone else is being unkind or making you feel bad, the best thing to do is walk away. Don't say angry words back. Talk about feelings in a safe way. Apologies are not ever in a forced hug. I did encourage handshakes, however. I would tell my kids, "You don't have to hug, you can give a high five or a hug, whichever you choose." Even if someone gives you a piece of candy, you never have to give a hug for that. It's always, "My body, my space."

To tell our kids that because someone did something nice for you, then you owe them a physical gesture sets up skewed expectations they can carry into adulthood. You reciprocate with your tone, with your voice, with your words, but there is nothing physically that you have to do for other people because they were kind to you.

There was one instance when we were at a social gathering with people we knew. Ailsa was about three years old and had always been taught she could hug or high five. She was close to me, but kind of wandered away, when I heard her yell, "No!" I looked over and there was a man trying to hug her. He was trying to grab her but was also hugging another little girl. He was crouched down, pulling the little girl into him. Nothing overtly criminal, but it gave me a weird feeling.

So I walked over and said, "Hey, what's going on?" I kept my tone calm and even.

"She won't give me a hug."

I looked to my daughter and said, "Well she gets to choose who she gives a hug to."

"Oh it's just a hug," he says, trying to turn it into a laughing matter.

"Ailsa, do you want to hug him?" I asked my daughter.

"No."

"She has made a decision. You don't get to hug her." I placed my daughter in a position where she is in control of her own body. It was interesting how many adults around me at this social gathering were like, "What's the big deal?" I had to reaffirm that she has her own body and her own mind, so she gets to make her own decisions.

What's the big deal? The big deal is that she felt something, and that feeling told her to say no. If I teach her to squelch that no, what am I really preventing my child from doing? People will try to use that shame to manipulate her boundaries. I want my children to grow up to be self-aware and responsible for their actions.

Sometimes my son would say, "I dunno what happened, I just hit him."

I would reply, "Of course you know what happened. This is your arm. The arm smacked him. Why, son?"

So there's that spectrum of you get to say no because you are responsible for your body, but you also have to take ownership when you hit someone. You don't get to say, "I don't know what happened."

Well, let's figure it out. This foot is attached to this ankle, which is attached to this leg, which is attached to . . . oh, yes, it's you! You kicked her. So you have to figure out why. You are responsible for hurting that other person. It helps to teach them, "Don't hurt, or don't let others hurt you," which is a much better motto than "Only say nice things" when it comes to this topic. As a result, I have a six-foot teenage son that doesn't accidentally hit people.

I taught my children that they never have to give a hug, they can choose to give a high five. Even if it's Mommy's really close friend, if you have a bad feeling, you don't have to be nice and you leave that situation. If it's a conflict with friends, you don't have to be part of that conversation. And if you are being hurt physically, you leave, and I will always back you up. Mom will always be on your side.

That was as close as we got to talking about sexual abuse at a young age.

Janet's Story

One of my friends told me her story. We will call her Janet.

"When I was ten, I was sexually molested by my twelve-year-old cousin. The first contact was a sleepover between my two brothers, him, and me. I was so awkward at that age I didn't know what to do, so I pretended I was asleep, even though I was fully aware of what was happening. My younger brother was even lying right next to me. Other molestations continued for about three to six months, with me always pretending to sleep, going to sleep in my parents' bedroom, or finding other ways to separate myself from him.

"I finally got the nerve to tell my mom. We were sitting on her bed alone when I told her what had been happening. Her initial reaction was, 'Oh honey, do you think you dreamed this? Are you sure you aren't making this up?' Of course I wasn't! I told her I have no reason to lie or make this up whatsoever. She told me she would have to tell my aunt. She relayed that when telling said aunt she confronted her son and he denied it. Of course he did. No twelve-year-old wants to get in trouble for touching his younger girl cousin inappropriately. So then my mom thought it would be a good idea to have a meeting with all four of us. We were at a family dinner and went to the basement, the exact room where an encounter had happened, and had this awkward talk. I don't even remember what was said. Possibly him apologizing and I said it's okay? Then at the end my mom also thought it was a good idea for me and him to *hug*. So that had to happen as well.

"From then on, no one spoke of it in my family. Time helped heal my wounds, but only through my Heavenly Father was I able to overcome this experience. My relationship with Him is undeniable and has helped me tremendously.

"I hope to share my knowledge, so my children won't ever have to experience something like this. I won't allow my kids to ever have a sleepover, because the parents can be vigilant but once they are asleep the kids might become curious." –Janet #metoo

Tree Analogy or You heard What?

When my son was eight years old, he was exposed by a neighbor boy to a conversation that we felt he was too young to handle. Obviously, we'd had the talk about your body is your own, don't let other people touch your body, and we had followed the Boy Scouts of America guidelines on what conversations to have with your children.

So, only my son and I were driving when he told me the neighbor boy had explained to him the concept of masturbating, along with the disturbing idea that if you force your penis into a girl, then she really likes it, even if she says no.

I just about drove us off the road.

We pulled over on the side of the road. I took a moment to be grateful that his younger sister was not also in the car. Then, I looked out the window and saw a tree that was dead. Right next to it was a tree that was green and beautiful. I pointed to the dead tree and asked, "Nathaniel, what is that?"

"It's a tree."

Then I pointed to the live tree and I said, "Nathaniel, what is that?"

"It's a tree," he said in all his eight-year-old wisdom.

I pointed back to the dead tree and I asked him what fun things we could do with that dead tree. We talked about how it could be really good for Halloween since it had a kind of spooky look. I pointed out that it didn't have any leaves. He was learning about photosynthesis in school, so I asked what it *wasn't* doing.

"It isn't giving us any air."

"So what is going to happen to a dead tree?"

"Well, someone is going to come and chop it down." We talked about how that tree won't give any shade, it wouldn't be fun to climb, and it doesn't give us any air.

Then I pointed to the live tree and asked what that was good for. We talked about how we could climb it and we could come have a picnic in its shade, yes with crackers and cheese. The conversation went on for so long that I almost thought that I'd be able to get out of the uncomfortable topic. So I took another deep breath.

"Nathaniel, they're both called trees, but their purpose and their use is very different." I let him kind of soak that up for a moment. "Nathaniel, what your friend was talking about is called sex. How did you feel when he was talking about sex?" Checking in with their feelings was how I tried to give my children the defenses they would need if they were to ever come up against an abuser.

After Nathaniel stated that he felt uncomfortable when this boy was talking to him about sex, and I validated his bad feeling. "Son," I said, "what you just heard about is the wrong kind of sex. It's like that dead tree, it's dead sex. When you force yourself on someone, is that good or is that bad? When you push someone to force them to sit down, is that good or is that bad?"

I tried to draw a parallel to the playground and how he understood the right and the wrong way to interact with others. When you force others to do things, it makes you feel bad inside.

"Nathaniel, dead sex leads to people feeling sad about themselves. It leads to them not feeling special or unique."

As my children have grown, I've been able to set up the vocabulary of dead sex and good or live sex. When they have questions about what happens on a movie screen, I'm able to show how dead sex leaves that person feeling used and not special. I explain that what their dad and I have is live sex and special; it's something beautiful between us, which is why we don't talk about it. Not because we're ashamed of it, but because it's private. And for people who do talk about it, they're trying to get validation from you.

With live sex, you can build a treehouse. You can create a home and life that fulfills you. When a mother and father create a family, that family gives back to the world, just like a live tree produces the air that we breathe and sometimes fruit we can eat.

The Bible teaches that, "By their fruits ye shall know them." (Matthew 7:20) Teach that by the fruits of the dead tree that dead sex is bad. It leaves people feeling vulnerable, emotional, and sad. Those fruits are not good.

As we talked that day in the car, Nathaniel asked a few more questions, then eventually got to the big one.

"Mom, how does it happen?"

Still not giving him more information than he needed to know, I asked, "Well what do you think happens?"

He had put all the information together and said to me that a penis goes into a vagina. I confirmed that was correct. He then said, "Mom, I think I'm going to need to watch you and Dad do it so I know that I'm doing it right."

Seriously.

"Son, that's the beautiful thing about being human," I explained. "When the time is right, you'll have all these hormones and emotions that will teach you what to do. And if you delay when you want to do it, until it's the right time to do it, then you will know everything that you need to know. And you don't need to watch anyone."

Like my experience with Nathaniel, most likely the open conversation you need to have with your children will be needed before you're ready for it to happen. As Nathaniel and Ailsa came home from school with other information, I'm always able to set up the conversation as, "Is that what your Dad and I have? Or is that dead sex?" And framing it that what their dad and I have is wonderful and awesome helps them distinguish between the right and wrong ways of sex and wanting the same physical intimacy in their mature relationships. It has been rewarding to see that my children want what we have, another impetus to keeping our marriage strong.

That conversation also helps protect them from imagery that children shouldn't be shown, against people touching them in inappropriate places, and to not engage in activities for which they aren't emotionally ready. You can also infuse that with your own beliefs.

Informed Consent

The constant bombardment of sexual innuendo in social media, movies, TV, video games and all other media numbs us until we start to think that sex is just an instinct and we should act upon our urges. This notion starts a slippery slope and blurs the lines until we have to argue about what consent actually means. Some very well-known people became so comfortable with acting on urges, they did not think enough about consent and now find themselves without a job. Sex without mutual consent has consequences, even years later.

There must always be informed consent. Children cannot provide consent because they are not informed of the consequences. So what is the age of consent? If you're applying to date my daughter, I say never. Okay, seriously, I don't feel qualified to propose an appropriate age. It is not my right to require a standard for others or to judge, but I do think that true love and commitment should be part of consent for any sexual act.

Intimacy has steps that lead toward sex. The steps are hands touching, hand holding, hugs, back rubs, cuddling, pecks, kissing, prolonged kisses, French kissing, fondling of privates, stimulation of the vagina and/or penis, and penis entering any body part. When my son was old enough, I taught him that each step you move up will leave your partner on that step, and the next person will be able to get to that step much quicker than you did. You don't want to take her to any step for which you are not committed to her with respect. As a teenager, I hope he will stay on the lower steps. As a man, I hope that he will go through other steps only after marriage. It is important to teach your children about these steps, how to give and ask for informed consent, and the consequences of proceeding through these steps too quickly. However, I caution you to avoid associating shame and guilt with going up the stairs, only that respect, informed consent, and commitment should accompany such acts. Telling kids sex is gross and dirty just leads them to kissing in a car one moonlit night thinking, "Mom and Dad are so dumb, they must not be doing it right!" Also, if shame is attached to sexual desires, when they get married, how can we expect that suddenly everything will be okay? It creates intimacy whiplash! "Wait, what, now I can? Huh?"

It is important we are clear: it is in the murky, shamed, and uninformed areas that evil acts are perpetrated on countless victims. If we are clear with our older children about the steps of intimacy, then they can decide where to draw their boundaries and how to give informed consent.

I do expect my children to live lives of abstinence from stimulating their private parts until marriage. I don't think they will go to hell if they don't. I tell my son, "If you 'experiment' on a girl, God will forgive, but it will take me longer." We still need to teach our children that if they mess up, the Atonement of Jesus Christ is there to take over. Often as parents we unwittingly put shame into something that is the most natural thing in the world. I teach them to wait so that they will be emotionally and mentally clear in their dating and ultimately in selecting who will be the parents of my amazing grandchildren.

For me, there is an ideal road that I want my children to travel. However, just like God, I hope to be understanding and loving should they choose a different route. I want them to be on this road because it allowed me to navigate dating and selecting my hubby, unencumbered by the thrills and pitfalls of sex without commitment. I considered myself a virgin of consent. When I chose to give myself to my husband, I could do so fully, and it has been amazing, deeply joyful, bonding, and beyond the words I can write in a book. I am able to trust my husband, knowing that he has the capacity for physical restraint, and he knows the same about me. In this fact alone, it makes what MTDMI did to me very different than what my husband and I have and makes any comparison between the two a disgusting suggestion.

Teach your children that when sex is a secret, it will hurt someone. And it's ironic that something a person may believe is so intimate and private is the gossip that will spread like wildfire. If sex is a secret, then there is something wrong with that relationship or experience. It is not a secret who I sleep with. I am not ashamed of it; I am proud of the man to whom I am married. When two people really love each other, they don't have a problem letting the world know and they don't need a Hollywood producer to set the stage.

Body Shame

I'm stepping out of the tub in my dripping-wet glory. My daughter was seven and she saw me and said, "Ewwww." My immediate reaction was, *Come on, I've had kids. I'm not that bad. Yes, I love my chocolate, but...*

I took a deep breath, stepped out like I was a Queen, and said, "Are you talking about this beautiful body? This incredible body that can do amazing things? That fed you and birthed you?" I went on and on, talking about all the amazing things that my body can do.

She was like, "Okay, whatever mom."

The strain we have about our own body shame sets our kids up to not understand boundaries. If we feel good about ourselves, then we communicate to our children that they are unique and special. I believe that we are each divine sons and daughters of God, and that our own imperfections are what add to our cuteness.

If we are uncomfortable with our own selves, we are teaching our children to be uncomfortable with their bodies. If an abuser gets ahold of that body shame, then the abuser knows that she can dig into that shame and create a deeper, more harmful shame.

Here's the ugly truth. If certain parts of our body are touched, it will feel good. If they are touched by you or an abuser, it will feel good. But the internal Speaker of Truth will let us know something isn't right if it is in the wrong place at the wrong time.

For a child being touched, it doesn't feel physically bad. Emotionally and mentally it feels bad, but most likely the abuser has already worked on the child's psychological doubts. But it doesn't hurt like a dog bite hurts you. Then the abuser will manipulate those emotions that come into, *if I didn't think it hurt then it must be okay. But my emotions are telling me this is wrong, so I must be wrong. Or I must be bad. Or I am doing what's wrong.*

This is something that I see a lot, in myself and in other abused individuals. Because it didn't hurt me like it did when I was hit, it was very confusing.

Summer at the Grand Canyon

I left two days after high school graduation to take a job on the North Rim of the Grand Canyon. It was a very relaxed atmosphere where literally everyone was having sex except me and one other girl. This one other girl had been raised on the bottom of the Grand Canyon. Her family had a little cabin without any running water. And it seemed we were the only two not having sex.

I was still healing from my years of abuse, and silently exploring what consent meant to me. Most of my co-workers respected my personal standard. There was one co-worker who didn't. As I was finishing one of my nightshifts, part of my duties was to dump the trash. When I was out back by the dumpster, he came up behind me and held a knife to my throat. He then proceeded to explain the sexual acts he expected from me.

What he didn't know is that I had been trained in martial arts. The boy was soon on the ground with his own knife at his throat. I called out and one of my friends on the night crew heard me and came. Ironically, the would-be-rapist was more physically damaged than I was. As I held the knife at his throat, I was calm as I assessed the threat he posed. However, once back in my little log cabin after the police interviews, I laid on my bed shaking as the adrenaline wore off and I considered what could have happened.

There was a different girl who joined our group later. She was so naive that she didn't know that boys knew about periods. She was horrified that men knew about girl stuff! She was suddenly thrown into an environment where people were getting drunk nightly, having casual sex and sexual harassment wasn't even a thing that shouldn't be in the work place. Sadly, she left that summer pregnant.

She had no defenses. Naïveté is not a defense. She was caught up in the thrill of a different lifestyle, but her lack of preparation put her in a position of reacting, instead of choosing what boundaries she wanted to enforce.

You can choose to be innocent. If there's a conversation that I'm uncomfortable with, I've learned to say, "Hey, I'm too young to hear that." It's something that I still say. We can choose to be innocent by what we choose to participate in but being ignorant removes your ability to build defenses. We need to be comfortable talking to our kids. They are going to get the information, let's have them get the information from us, including age-appropriate explanations.

So in review of what we can do as parents to protect our children from abuse:

1. Don't get all weird when talking about body parts. Head, shoulders, vagina, penis, knees, and toes are all parts of our body.
2. Body responsibility means you get to clean it, but you can also choose yourself who you hug and who you don't.
3. Talk with your kids about everything they want to talk about. The reward will be they will talk to you about everything.
4. Remove shame and don't label a kid as bad or certain parts as bad. Explain that private means that those body parts are used in privacy.
5. Identify the usefulness of the feeling as a good or bad source
6. Teach your kids awareness as appropriate by age, without scaring them.

Chapter 18

Holding up the Good

"For me it was my own father...my mother blamed me for 'ruining her life.'" –Sandi Stillings #metoo

SOME TIME AGO I WAS on a professional phone call with a man who kept calling me "Sweetie." Very politely, I told him that I didn't care for his word choice, but I appreciated that he felt close enough to me to use that term of endearment. I was giving him the benefit of the doubt, because I was pretty sure he was using that word to put me down.

"Now Sweetie," he said, "there's no need to get all upset." I reinforced that this was a professional setting, and I would prefer to keep things professional. I then ended the conversation.

My daughter overheard that phone call. This set us up to have a conversation about how I only allow my husband to use those special terms of endearment with me. I told her that even though I go by "Hotness" on social media, if a man messages me and says, "Hey, you're hot," then I immediately block him. I told her that I have something special that I reserve for my husband. I value my relationship with him over anyone else who may want to stroke my ego.

When we aren't willing to hold up the good, the bad can over-power it. It seems that most media teach that the way to communicate with another human being is through touch. And even though sex is awesome, what's even more awesome is having sex with someone that you know likes you, loves you, respects you, values you, and puts you above all others. That is amazing. It's so great, that I can tell you why MTDMI has never been in my marriage bed. Even though the physical acts were the same, the intent behind them was so different. My husband has never touched me without love. He has never wanted me to satisfy his own perversion. Everything from MTDMI was about selfishness, gratification, and evil.

Once I was in my survival phase—the abuse had stopped, and I was trying to sort through everything that had happened—I was very confused because I wasn't in a hospital bed battered and beaten. I fig-ured there must have been some love in it. We do that as individuals, comparing our own experiences to someone else's trauma.

I would hear about molestations that were brutal, and of course, my heart went out to such victims. For a long time I was confused because I wasn't chained up, it didn't leave a scar or physical mark on my body that said I had been mishandled. I was told it was love. I was told it was natural. It's definitely not natural for a man who is almost forty and a girl who wasn't even fourteen.

After my wedding, the first night that my husband took me in his arms and showed me how much he loved me was so tender and beautiful, unlike anything it had been with MTDMI. My husband was there to show me how much he loved me: it wasn't for any type of selfish gratification, and he was very aware of me physically, emo-tionally, and mentally. He had already chosen to show that he could curb his sexual desires and wait for me, for our marriage to have this special moment.

Are we teaching our children what real love is? Or, do they think that sex is about physical gratification, sexuality, and desire? Love that lasts is about kindness, service, patience, forgiveness, and working together. Sex becomes the cherry on top, the fun thing you get to do.

When I was in a wheelchair because of my pregnancies, my husband did not turn away from me. He still complimented me. He did not become mean because his sexual needs were not being met, he did not find another source to satisfy his "urges." His emotional, mental, and spiritual needs were being met. We love each other, and we worked through that challenge together.

They say married couples fight the most about money and sex, but the truth is probably that there are things that weren't working before those fights come up. Our children are watching our marriages. If you act like two people who are stuck together, then they'll start creating blueprints of what marriage and love is like. But if you show them that there is something this good and this amazing out there, then you can insulate them against abusers who will twist what love is.

MTDMI twisted a lot of things that my parents taught me about sex, but he could never twist what I saw. I credit two couples for showing me that marriage could be a beautiful thing. One couple is my parents. They flirted in ways that was disgusting to us kids but was actually really sweet. I knew, at a very young age, that my parents enjoyed each other sexually, as communication partners, and as business partners. They didn't show us things or talk about it, but just their glances at each other, the touches, told us a lot. When my dad would get home after days of driving trucks, we all knew that they got some alone time together. Thankfully my parents held up the good for me.

The second couple I credit were my neighbors, Rita and Paul Debry. I knew they also loved each other. It was never inappropriate, but there was teasing and reaching for each other. These two couples were my earliest clues that the molestation that was happening to me was not okay.

If you complain to your children about your spouse, you tear down their ideals of what love could be. They need to see you united and working through differences together. When there is a dysfunctional marriage shown to children, if that child is being abused, they can come to understand that love and sex are not good.

We have power as parents to show our children that marriage is about enhancing each other emotionally, psychologically, financially, spiritually, and physically. When one of these areas starts to break down, we need to fix it, because that's a kink that an abuser can use. Because I had been shown love by my parents, by my father, it wasn't hard for me to imagine a God that loved me. And if you are reading this and don't believe in God, I can understand that too, because there were times when I couldn't imagine Him either. But even in my darkest times when I blamed God, when I talked to Him in angry tones or told Him all the mistakes He had made, He always replied back in love. That answer came at different times, sometimes soon, or the next day, or at some other point when I was brushing my teeth. But the answer is always so clear, and exactly what I needed to hear, that I know that it didn't come from me. I would be ungrateful to not acknowledge His hand in my life.

I want those of you reading this to know that our God is a loving God. Our God is a good God. Bad things happen because humans live here. God never intended for what happened to me to happen. He never wanted those who have endured private sexual abuse, or public abuse, or any other form of physical, mental, or emotional abuse to happen. That is not from God, but from the ill use of agency of God's children. Our God is comfortable hearing anything that we have to say. Does He like seeing bad things happen? No. But I've also seen Him take what's bad and replace it with wisdom and strength.

As parents, we need to act toward our children like God might toward His children. When we hear ugly, or anger, or unkind things from our children, we need to respond how He would. God responds in kindness, in patience, and when needed, in vengeance. When you make mistakes, apologize to your children. Your kids will make mistakes, too, and will learn that saying sorry is a sign of maturity.

The major turning points in my life have come after talking to God. It's so clear that God wants to hear all of this from us that we as parents need to be comfortable talking about everything. When our children come to us with questions about pornography or masturbation, and we're uncomfortable with these topics, they will keep looking for answers until they find some. Who do you want to be the one answering those questions? Who do you want to be the one imprinting on their minds what love is? Show them that life can be good. And if they see that your life isn't good, have them watch you fighting for a good one. Let them see you taking a stand for something good, and always make sure to hold up the good that is in your marriage, your relationship with God, or in your life.

Chapter 19

Teach Truth Over Kindness

"Words: So innocent and powerless as they are, as standing in a dictionary, how potent for good and evil they become in the hands of one who knows how to combine them."
–Nathaniel Hawthorne

THERE IS AN OLD SAYING, "If you can't say anything nice, don't say anything at all." Children don't often understand the nuances of what this phrase is trying to say. What we're trying to tell our children is to be kind. What we're trying to tell our children is not to say mean things to random strangers. As any mother knows, children are apt to go say harsh things to strangers because they see things literally.

I remember once my daughter pointed at someone and said, "Wow, she's really fat." I was mortified. I was absolutely mortified. I had no idea she knew that word. That lady heard it, and I cried inside for her. I went over and apologized. She told me it was fine because she hears it from kids all the time. I touched her on the arm and said it didn't matter, that she is a human being, and I proceeded to grovel in apology. Then I had a conversation with my daughter that if we see something that is different or unique about someone to think about if it would help them to say it. In a way, that reiterates "If you can't say anything nice, don't say anything at all," but it is important to teach our children how to talk to strangers.

Another time I was with my son and he said, "Mom! Look! That man doesn't have a leg!" The man heard and his body language made him appear that he was open to talking about it. Again I walked over to the man.

"I see that you heard my son is intrigued by your missing leg," I said. "I assume there must be a story to go with that. Do you mind sharing it with us?" The man proceeded to tell us how he lost it in a motorcycle accident and told my son to avoid motorcycles. I went ahead and agreed with his advice.

In both of these embarrassing situations, the way that I hopefully lessened the hurt was by talking to these people. I didn't just hush my child and say, "Shh! Don't say that!" Although embarrassed, by talking to both of these people, I taught my children that there is a person there, a person behind that thing that you noticed.

I have been made fun of for having a moustache (thank you laser hair removal). Growing up, I was teased for not having all of my teeth due to a thrilling bicycle accident. When someone is made fun of for a physical appearance, I'm really sensitive to that because I was made fun of for so many years. When my daughter made that heartless comment at the young age of three, it was because she had not experienced being made fun of for her looks. It didn't occur to her that might be a hurtful thing because it was out of her frame of reference.

Bringing this back to teaching our children about sexual safety, if I'm teaching my child not to say things, then I'm teaching my child she does not have a voice. If she doesn't have a voice, does she not have value? These are strange nuances in a child's mind. It may seem like a far leap from shushing your child in the grocery store for saying something unkind, but in my own story and in those of many victims that I have talked with, we did not speak up because we knew it was "unkind." It was uncomfortable.

I believe that saying uncomfortable things is especially difficult for women in our society. If a man speaks his mind, he is called bold, assertive, or a leader. If a girl is outspoken, they might call her unladylike if she's lucky, but most likely will be called a witch or a word that sounds like it. When women are assertive, it's a problem. I think this goes back to our cultural roots that women are to be demure and attractive. I think it's innate in many women to desire to be attractive, but when you couple that with the Victorian notion that women are also to be the keepers of virtue, you start tracing it back to these ideas that children are to be seen, not heard. At its root, we only wanted to teach our children to be kind, but isn't it more important to teach our children to speak the truth?

Let's think about that.

We do not want our kids going up to people and saying they're fat, but we do want our kids to say someone is touching my body when I've been told that I am in charge of my body. So how do we draw that line? Where are the nuances of what truth to tell to whom?

We're teaching our children that we don't want to say things that will hurt people's feelings, yet so many bad things happen in our society because people are silent. I cannot think of any secrets that are empowering. I can't think of a situation where not telling the truth is good, except maybe a surprise birthday party, but eventually the truth will come out.

Any time we teach our kids to keep secrets, it's a problem for everything, not just sexual abuse. It's even a problem for kindness. Let me explain that.

We all remember American Idol, the singing show that was extremely popular in the early 2000s (and alas, the show continues today with perhaps less popularity). People come try out for American Idol, and they stand up on that stage and sing. Some are so bad that there is an entire reality show based around how terrible they are at singing, to contrast against those who are quite good and may advance or even win. How do these bad singers get to this point in life where they were willing to stand up in front of critical judges and all of America? Why did no one tell them they were bad at singing?

Barring any mental handicap or manipulation, I have to assume that it's because their parents were the type that handed out trophies for participation. These are the people that show up to jobs and expect one million dollars, or that since they've been around the longest they deserve the perks. How do they become so self-deceived? They become self-deceived because no one actually rose their hand and said, "No, um...you're not actually right here." Their thinking or self perceptions have never been challenged.

We all have that crazy aunt we humor, and no one actually says the truth to her. We think it's kindness, but then she goes out in the world and deals with other people and is shocked when they don't comply with her dysfunction, so she stays in the circles that allow her to behave poorly. Is that really kindness? Is allowing someone to remain self-deceived really helping that person?

Now I don't think I have it all sorted out in my own life on how to handle these situations. But when it comes to this topic, I am so against teaching anyone that silence is a goal. How is silence anything good? Bad things happen when good people stay silent. When you look at the breakdowns in societies and cultures, it all comes from the concept of "Shhh." Indeed, ignoring consequences of behavior does not mean that those consequences still do not exist.

Are children capable of understanding the nuanced difference between being politely quiet and speaking up against potentially dangerous behavior? I say no. Teach your children to tell the truth; then, when they say embarrassingly unkind things like "She's really fat," teach them to talk to that person and discover that there is more than what they just see. Teach that child to interact with those people who may seem different than them, to appreciate those differences, and to learn to love other people.

Teach our children that what they have to say is okay; that what they are feeling is okay, and it's just how they choose to express themselves that makes them more mature. As a child, you might say things that aren't nice because you're still working on your communication skills, but it's important to say the truth. Teach truth. Truth is more important than kindness. I know it seems crazy. I trumpet kindness! But not at the cost of truth.

The formula is that when we feel sticky, we need to teach our children to use their words. When my kids were in fights, I would direct them back to how they felt. The awesome feelings came from God and the bad feelings came from Satan. You can label those feelings however you need to, but teach kids to recognize the difference. When they feel that contention, hurt, and anguish, they can always speak to us. If your child is being molested or bullied, don't you want to know? Or would you rather they only say kind things? If it doesn't leave a smile when I say it, then I shouldn't say it—is that more important than the truth?

To reiterate, teach our children to speak the truth, then teach them to be kind. Be a safe place for children to talk, to express their feelings and know that you won't get angry. Teach them to keep their inner voice talking by always listening to it.

Chapter 20

Use More Sympathy and Empathy

"The world is a dangerous place, not because of those who do evil, but because of those who look on and do nothing."
–Albert Einstein

THINKING YOU UNDERSTAND SOMEONE'S MOTIVATIONS and way of thinking without actually talking to them puts you in a place of judgement. Why would you put yourself in that situation when you should be figuring out you? Look around and see all these things that you can connect with other people on if you just drop the labels.

We are told to not judge, but of course we need to make judgements all the time. How else can we decide where to place a person in our Circle of Intimacy? We are judging a person's ability to love, be accountable, and be trustworthy to know where to place that person in our rings.

It's a tricky line to not become biased toward a certain group of people while still making judgments that will keep us safe. The formula that I give is sympathy = conversation + kindness. When you start to feel resentment toward a person because they are different, as a parent you can walk your child up to that person and help your child get to understand that person, and perhaps come to learn why they are different.

Now I get it, it may not always be safe to walk your child up to everyone. One day we were downtown in our metro area and my son saw a homeless man having an animated conversation with his Coca-Cola® can. That is not a situation where I would take my son over there. I mean, first of all, it's just rude to interrupt.

My son was around ten years old. "Why is that happening?" he asked. Instead of turning him around and shushing him, we talked about mental illness.

"Nathaniel, some people have had such horrible things happen to them, that it mentally breaks them, and they are never the same again."

After that conversation, he decided that he wanted to raise money for the homeless, which he did. We reframed the conversation from, "That person took drugs, and because he took drugs he's now on the street," to we don't know what happened. Maybe he took drugs to escape from the things that were really bad and horrid. How many victims out there are looking for that escape? In my mind, thousands of people died when the Goblin Guy attacked my kingdom. In a way, taking drugs may have been nicer or easier.

Nathaniel now saw that since he was not on the side that had that problem, he was on the other side that needed to help. It gave him a tender spot for the homeless. Throughout his young life, he has sought opportunities to be kind to everyone. When I'm walking downtown, I do not give out money, but occasionally we have given out water bottles with notes on them or some kind of food.

Hate comes from judgment. Judgment comes from a lack of empathy. A lack of empathy comes from not talking to people. Teach children that we are all of value. Because if anyone, anyone, does not have value, then our children are not safe. Think about it. Think about the ramifications if each person in our neighborhood or city felt valued, and even better, loved.

I was at a networking conference and we were told to answer the question, "What is the worst thing that has happened to you?" Now, when I'm asked something like this, I usually don't tell them the real thing.

I'm at a table when a lady began her story, "My daughter got really sick." When I heard those words, and I saw the look in her eye, I got up from my seat and put my arm around her. When she had to say, "Then my daughter died," she had my comfort, and she knew that I had also buried a child. We had empathy for each other. The other women at the table were able to have sympathy and kindness for us. But because of our shared experiences, this woman and I became instant friends.

A woman expressed her surprise that we were so close, because, to her, we seemed so different. She started pointing out our differences like I'm religious and Trisha is not. I'm married to a man; she is married to a woman. But those labels weren't nearly as big as what we have in common. This woman chose to see the two of us by our labels, categorizing each of us as "they/them."

I have had people tell me that I am going to hell for belonging to my faith. It is easy for us in all faiths to look at those of a different faith and judge them. Well, I'm pretty sure that only God can determine that. Don't turn things into an-us-versus-them comparison. God says that judgement belongs to Him.

I had a conversation with a friend who described herself as non-religious and told me I was going to go to her version of hell.

"Why do you think I'm going to the void?"

"You don't eat the way you should." She informed me that by eating things from a can, I would go to hell. It was a very interesting discussion to go back and forth with each other and I was able to point out to her that she had her own religion that had its own version of damnation. Her mind was blown when she realized I was right. My mind was blown when she admitted I was right.

So how does this connect to our kids? When you're teaching your children to recognize that yucky feeling that something's not quite right, then teach them that when they have those feelings to come and talk to you. Then you can stop the bullying, you can stop the molestations, because you're teaching them to recognize their gut. I believe every single person has the light from God, but it gets pushed out of us through our different experiences. It gets pushed out of us when we're told "Shhh, don't talk! Other people can talk, but not you because you're not valuable."

So when children feel this conflict because they have this light inside them that tells them something is wrong but they are told by authority figures not to talk about uncomfortable things, they eventually give in and go silent. And not all of these children are molested. Some are bullied. Some aren't bullied or molested but become adults that are unfulfilled because they never learned to listen to themselves or to establish safe boundaries. Then those adults are the ones pointing out the "them" that deserve judgement, because that judgement comes from a place of shame.

If ever I catch myself in this cycle of judgment, it's something of which I immediately repent. It's human nature to make judgments, but we don't have to accept that as our best self. We have to fight it. If ever I find myself making judgments about a group of people, that's when we can say that we should go learn more about them.

I was in Indonesia for a speaking engagement and my hosts wanted to take me to Bali. I was all for it! They took me to a resort that's marble as far as you can see until it stops and frames the Indian Ocean perfectly. The Indian Ocean! That was pretty cool for a girl who grew up in the Mountain West. There were monkeys everywhere. I had an amazing, five-star experience. My mind was in that place of being pampered.

As we were leaving this beautiful resort, we had to go through a rough part of the city at night. My hosts were explaining to me that there was a lot of prostitution in this area. I looked out my window and saw a boy that I thought was around thirteen. He pulled his ten-year-old sister by the hand and was dragging his five-year-old brother by the arm as they were attempting to cross a busy street. Enraged, I turned to my host and said, "Where is their mother?"

My host just looked at me. As we passed this boy in our fancy SUV, I made eye contact with him. What I saw haunts me still. He was completely dead inside. It was then I realized that his mother was probably a prostitute, and she wasn't there, so he had to be in charge of two other lives. Maybe he didn't even know his mother. If I had looked at him with kindness, instead of judging, maybe things could have been different. I may not be able to do much for his situation, but I could have at least rolled down the window and handed him the food I had with me.

My host explained to me that those children would most likely end up in the sex trade, and that some of the biggest leaders within the sex industry had been sex slaves themselves.

That hurts. That's really hard stuff. The truth of the matter is that what happened to me is not nearly as bad as what happens to many millions of people.

My experiences are different than your experiences. "Oh I know exactly how you feel." No you don't, but if we can communicate, you can get to a place where you can say, "I want to understand how you feel."

There's power that comes from stepping outside of your circle of people who think like you. I call it your mental inbreeding. If you never talk to someone that challenges your belief system, how will you know if your beliefs are true or are the best of what God has in store for you?

I tell my kids to not pick their friends from among those that believe exactly like them. I tell them to pick friends from people of good character. Who you hang out with absolutely rubs off on you, for good or for bad. Hang out with a gang, and you'll think the entire world is made up of gang bangers. I lived in Washington D.C. and worked as an interpreter in a hospital. I would talk to people who thought that because my skin was white nothing bad had ever happened to me, and because their skin was black, they had no choice but to be in a gang. It broke my heart. I tried to explain that if we talked we would have a lot more in common than they probably thought, but their perception was confined to this narrow box out of which they could not break.

I am proud that the friends my kids have chosen are not all just like them. They surround themselves with people among all religions and colors of skin. If they're surrounded by people who are pushing themselves to have new experiences and become their best selves, then they aren't going to be so set on the labels. My kids will have a richer experience in life because they won't see a mystical "them" out on the horizon to get them.

My friend Stacey McCarthy teaches her kids to join four things, and they have to mix the experiences or the genres. They can't join four sports. They can join three sports, and then the chess club. Or you can join three clubs and one sport. The point is to mix up the experiences and the friendships and connections you are making.

I love this idea. As I have contemplated the formula that I used to get to my place of healing, and as I have talked with other victims, all of them have referenced getting outside their immediate circle that was handed them. For me, my religious community was a huge aspect of me realizing that what was happening was not okay. They gave me resources and people and connections that were a saving grace for me.

When I look back on my happiest times of life, it's when I've been involved in a variety of different things, surrounded by a circle of diverse people. Encouraging our children to diversify their acquaintances will help them figure out what they really believe because they will actually get to talk about it. Don't push the idea that agreement is valuable, or that we have to all agree in order to like each other. Really, that just leads to a lot of hate. What if you're in a situation where everyone agrees that you should get punched?

Going back to what my friend Stacey has said about joining four things, I advocate that one of those four things needs to be service. If you belong to a church community, there's a lot of service there. If you don't, there are always service opportunities in your community. At least once a month you should be serving someone.

Within every religion, philosophy, life coach, success guru they'll tell you that service is integral to being happy. That's something that we can teach our kids. And, as we serve, we'll get new ideas and we'll gain more respect for people. When we respect people—not necessarily agree with them—then we won't demonize them. Imagine your child comes to you and says, "Susie was mean to me because she's a mean person." The mommy in you may want to go and punch Susie, but if you can sit down and have a conversation about what actually happened with Susie, you are teaching your child to understand the truth, which hopefully often leads to distinguishing good from bad, safe from unsafe. The most important truth is that they always have a voice, and how they use their words defines their kindness.

Sympathy, Empathy, and Ignorance

People can say stupid stuff. Like really mean things. Many of these stupid, mean things do come from hate, prejudice, rationalization, and sometimes fear. Far more often the dumb things we say to each other come from ignorance. We sometimes fail to see that, were the situation reversed, we could be just like them. Here's a list of really insensitive things we say about those who are victims of abuse, assault, molestation, sexual harassment, and sexuality. Sadly, this is by no means a complete list.

They should have known better.

You should have seen it coming.

You should expect harassment if you are_____.

Everyone is having sex, it's just human.

You have sex with your partner, so why is having sex with the rapist so hard on you?

If they were there, they were asking for it.

You shouldn't have been dressed sexy.

It's your fault because you_____.

Oh, it could have been worse!

I hope you get assaulted/raped.

If you were close to God, you would have been protected.

God only lets things happen if it is part of His plan.

You shouldn't have been drinking.

You shouldn't have been using drugs.

I remain in control of situations, so I am safe.

Men can't be raped, they like sex too much.

This is only a women's issue.

Didn't you try to fight back?

Dress in a modest way so others don't have bad thoughts about you.

They must not be a good person.

In time, you'll get over it (meaning the assault, rape, molestation) and even forget it ever happened.

Don't talk about it.

You manifested this or brought this upon yourself.

How long are you going to be sad about this? Just get over it!

Those people are just like that.

In the suburbs (or whatever you think makes you safe) we are safe.

Most people that say things like this aren't trying to be hurtful. Most likely these comments come from a lack of sympathy and empathy.

Sympathy: Suppose that I've lived in the Mountain West region my entire life (I haven't, but let's pretend this is true). I hear about a tsunami. Now, tsunamis don't happen where I live. These occur in places completely different from where I live. Places that have a different temperature, different atmosphere, and a whole different culture from my experience. But I'm sad when I hear about the tsunami. I might post something on my social media. I might write a check. If I'm really awesome, I might even go do some type of service project, like making hygiene kits. When I talk to a survivor of a tsunami, I feel sad. This is called sympathy.

Empathy: Suppose I have lived through a tsunami (again, I haven't, but let's pretend). When I hear about a tsunami happening, everything about my own experience resurfaces—the sights, the sounds, the smells. I am there, imagining the faces and the heartache of those who have just experienced something I have been through. I pick up the phone and relate with a survivor of this latest tsunami, and in doing so, I provide empathy.

Our brains are very fascinating. We want to relate to everything we hear. An example is when you're standing at a party and someone shares a story about getting a ticket. Then suddenly everyone is sharing their stories of getting pulled over. We share these experiences, and as human beings it's how we connect to each other. We find commonalities. Eventually, when you're talking to someone, you will find things you have in common and it is a really wonderful way to interact.

The flip side of that is that when we hear something that is not relatable to us and we don't want it to relate to us because it's bad, our brain will try to prevent that bad thing from happening to us. When I, as someone who has lived in the Mountain West, hear of a tsunami, I might start thinking things like, "I'm so glad I don't live in a place where tsunamis might happen." The slippery slope begins when we start thinking it was their fault for living in that area. That's a risk of which they should have been aware. They brought it on themselves.

However, in the Mountain West, we have the risk of earthquakes! In everything, there's some pros and some cons. There's always a "could've, should've, would've," but the truth is that every place you live has some risk to it. But our brains want to think that what we are choosing is the best, safest option. Otherwise our cortisol—a chemical that causes stress in the brain—would be released all the time, and we would have no enjoyment in our everyday situation.

One day while riding his road bike, my husband was hit by a bus. Yup, literally. Now, any time I hear about someone getting hit by a vehicle, my empathy is immediately activated. I know that is their worst day. I see the scars on my husband's body. Because of that experience, I have a greater understanding of, and ability to empathize with, those whose spouses are ill or injured. Because my husband had a heart attack, I'm right there with the 70-year-old ladies that have husbands with heart conditions. Because of the death of my child, there are people who look at me and say, "What did she do wrong to have that happen?" Sadly, this applies to every aspect of our lives.

Our brains want to insulate us from every bad thing. This also happens when we hear about someone being raped or sexually abused. "She should have known that person was an abuser." "He should have known not to go to that location or party." "She should have known not to wear that dress." "He shouldn't have been drunk."

It was fascinating to me to hear of the girl who was raped at Stanford University behind a dumpster. I was discussing it with someone who said, "Well she shouldn't have been that drunk."

"Don't you drink?" I asked.

"Well...yeah," she said.

I replied, "Every time you drink, are you accepting the liability that you may get raped and it would be your fault?"

We engage in behavior all the time that could get us killed. Like driving a car. But our brains have decided it's okay because we do it all the time, it isn't something to get stressed out about.

Sadly with abuse, statistics show us that it is not rare or uncommon. Why is this? I think some of the sources to blame is that we don't talk about it. We don't talk to our children about it enough to give them the weapons they need, such as noticing a red flag like when a trespasser is manipulative. We also need to empower them to say no to advances or to doing things that make them vulnerable. And learning some self-defense may make sense.

I don't fault my parents, but if I had been armed with knowledge, perhaps the abuse would have ended earlier. Or, it wouldn't have gotten to a physical stage. I'm sure the mental and emotional abuse would have still happened, and that was really where the most damage was done, but I would have been able to recognize it earlier.

Empathy comes from shared experience, but sympathy comes from a lack of judgment. If we don't give our children the right information, they may never be able to develop the empathy and sympathy needed to stop judging others. If we cut down on judgment, then when a victim comes forward, we can give him support instead of defaulting to our natural brain that says, "Well he should have..." We weren't there. We don't know. Our job as a society is to support the victim, and to get help or punishment for the abuser as needed. Our system right now is set up to protect the abuser. A child, *a child*, currently has to state the time, date, location, and who was involved. A five-year-old cannot tell you exactly where or when it happened.

But things are changing. The first step is talking about it, and I love that we are having more open and honest conversations.

Chapter 21

Secrets are Toxic

"I knew I was too young to be someone's girlfriend, but when I said that to him, he told me that that's why I couldn't tell anyone." –Makenna C. #metoo

PHRASES THAT ARE UNHEALTHY: "It's eating me up inside," "If I don't tell someone I'll explode," and "I just have to say something." These phrases are our gut telling us that secrets are not okay.

As this book came about, I had women come to me that were upset that I suddenly felt this need to speak up. Someone said, "That happened to me, too, but we don't need to talk about it." I was talking to a friend about this, and she said her mom had told her the same thing! Her mom had been molested and said she didn't think that was something that should be talked about openly.

It's another form of the idea that words should not be expressed. When you look at our society, a lot of our pain comes from not being able to talk about our feelings. In a conversation about sexual abuse, there is one party that thinks it's okay, and there is one party that is suppressing what they feel.

Secrets are bad. Teach that if anyone asks you to keep a secret long-term (unlike a surprise birthday party, which is going to become known to all involved), then that's wrong. I've told my kids that if someone ever tells them, "Don't tell your mom" then that's a warning sign. When our children tell us things that we preferred we didn't hear, try to not yell or get upset. Instead, ask what they're thinking. Open up lines of communication.

I know not every home is going to do this, but because every home won't do this, does that mean we won't even try? How heartbreaking it is to know of situations that some people are being raised in, but that doesn't mean that the rest of us shouldn't even try, because maybe it'll make a huge difference in the world of some kids that cross our paths or are exposed to our healthy family culture.

Less secrets. More truth. Seek to see each other with kindness.

Makenna's Story

"I was molested when I was about five years old. It was during the longest summer of my life. One specific boy, who lived across the road, took an interest in me. He was 11 or so and would always want to be my partner when we'd play hide and seek or have our "apple wars" in the woods. He made me feel important at first, like I belonged, like I should be there with them, but then his tone changed, and he began to tell me that I was his girlfriend. I knew I was too young to be someone's girlfriend, but when I said that to him, he told me that that's why I couldn't tell anyone. He told me that girlfriends have to touch their boyfriends, it's what makes them special.

"I didn't know that what was happening was wrong, or that I could have walked into my house, told my parents and it could have been over. Instead, I worked the rest of the summer to be a better "girlfriend" and make sure my abuser was pleased with me. Thankfully, (of what I can remember) my abuse only lasted one summer. In the fourth grade after a discussion with my mom about how someone tried getting her to do something bad when she was young, I finally said, 'Mom…that has happened to me.'

"My parents were amazing. They were on my team, they supported me and told me it wasn't my fault. They did all the right things. They notified the boy's parents, they took it to authorities, they got me into counseling. They helped tremendously.

"Unfortunately, this early experience led me on a long path of promiscuity and self destruction. In high school, I was known as easy. I was popular and happy on the outside, but tortured, depressed, miserable, and extremely vulnerable on the inside. I wouldn't even pray because I didn't think Heavenly Father cared about a girl who used her body the way that I did.

"I was fortunate to meet a man that didn't expect me to perform to make him happy. He later became my husband, and we returned to my childhood faith where we found goals that we worked toward and achieved together. The Lord helped me feel whole again. He helped me know that what happened to me wasn't my fault, nor did it destroy my chances of being whole again.

"I still have hard days. I battle depression and anxiety and have been diagnosed with bipolar disorder. There are still memories of what was, that make me feel small and vulnerable again.

"My heart aches for the little girl he abused. I'm so sad for what she was exposed to and what she went through to get here. I look back at myself and sob because I remember how scary it was. I remember the smell of his breath, and how I knew something was getting ready to happen because of the specific look in his eye. I remember every place I was at when he enticed me to do things with him. I remember the conversations I had with myself to try and be a better "girlfriend". I should have *never* gone through that, but I did. Now I'm a parent who is aware and ready to discuss this with my children. This will not happen to them. I cannot let this happen to them." –*Makenna C. #metoo*

Secrets cannot and should not be kept. We are taught it is somehow disloyal to tell, however the real betrayal is to ourselves. Keeping secrets is literally damaging to our physical health, mental health and relationships.

> "Traumatized people chronically feel unsafe inside their bodies: The past is alive in the form of gnawing interior discomfort. Their bodies are constantly bombarded by visceral warning signs, and, in an attempt to control these processes, they often become expert at ignoring their gut feelings and in numbing awareness of what is played out inside. They learn to hide from their selves."[10]

My body held on to the years of suppression and then manifested it as an autoimmune disease. Many victims of abuse have other illnesses like bipolar, anxiety, depression, or other health issues. As I said before, not everyone who faces these challenges have been abused. But the mental, physical, and spiritual ramifications of abuse is why we can never look on sexual deviations casually. My friend Jeri sent this to me, it so well illustrates the destruction the untold secrets hold.

Jeri's Story

"It started with what I call the "Silent Scream". I would wake in the middle of the night to the most terrifying, blood curdling scream coming from my soul. It was deafening in my head, but not external. I couldn't breathe, I was literally gasping for air like I was being smothered. The only way I could justify it was maybe I'd had a bad dream or panic attack? I finally called to go in for a therapy session. It was then that I first heard the term "body memory". Sometimes the memories that our body stores are not always memories that we consciously remember. You may have been too young to remember, or maybe you blacked out. However, your body is capable of storing memories too, as opposed to only the brain.

---

10   Bessel A. van der Kolk, *The Body Keeps the Score: Brain, Mind, and Body in the Healing of Trauma* (Penguin Books, 1997) 97.

"After months of counseling sessions, my therapist told me she thought there was something deeper going on in my subconscious and recommended hypnosis. I refused, so she suggested I speak to family members and ask questions about my childhood, since I truly did not remember most of it. When I started asking questions, my mother first answered with silence, and then finally the story came out. I had been sexually abused by my paternal grandfather from the age of two, yes you read that correctly, two years old. I was a toddler and it continued until I was four. My step-grandmother is the one that brought it to light as she had suspected it for a long time. He, the man that most little girls look up to and admire and trust and want love from, violated little me in unthinkable ways.

"Once "The Scream" was released from my subconscious, the memories started coming back rapidly. It was so frightening. I was forty years old and would literally curl up like a baby in fear, panic and internal pain. My little daughter brought me her teddy bear, saying, "Mommy, maybe he will make you feel better."

"The journey to get to the other side was really tough. My dad refused to believe it, as he had way back then, or couldn't believe it because it was his father who did it. Not until a few years later did he come to me with a very tearful, heartfelt apology when he found out for himself that even as a dying man, his father was still watching child porn. My cousin came forward at the funeral and told my father, "He did it to me too".

"There are so many, many details and terrible parts to my story, but I am free, seriously free now! It was worth the pain, agony, anger, hate, divorces (twice), to get to where I am today. I can tell you that my saving grace was my relationship with my God. He sustained me and gave me peace. He taught me that I was *loved* beyond measure and He is the one that opened my heart and unfolded my future to possibilities of love, acceptance, forgiveness, and even joy!

"Little Jeri is at peace now and Big Jeri has blossomed into all (well at least I'm getting there) I was created to be. Very few know of this side of me, because it is *not* what defines me. Yes it happened, but it's just my past. I look forward, not behind, and I look for all the blessings to come that are for me. Those that know me now hear me say quite frequently that I love my life, and I truly do. For all that it is, good and bad, it is mine. Now I choose to live life the way I want and not have it defined by what happened to me.

"I am not a victim, I am victorious! I am blessed!"

—Jeri Taylor-Swade #metoo

When a secret spills out somehow, it's usually not in a helpful way. It is better to rip the mask off and expose it for what filth it is. Yes it may be hard, but how much is lost to shame now in our cumulative silence? I am so glad that Jeri is able to heal now, but perhaps the body memories wouldn't have been so painful if she'd been able to work through her trauma earlier. I'm not blaming her family, as that is an awful situation, but secrets are never a helpful or healthy thing.

I originally heard this analogy from Ken Patey, who runs GrowthClimate in Utah. He talks about how people are like onions. Once you find out what really motivates you, you can strip away all the other layers, cry, and realize why you do everything that you do. We hide things in the onion layers, which is okay. It would not be okay for me to walk around introducing myself as, "Hi, I'm Leta Greene. I buried a child, I had a pretty dysfunctional childhood, I have a chronic illness. Oh, did I mention the PTSD? Yeah don't forget that. But it's all good because I have a happy marriage and functioning kids." That's a weird introduction, right?

I've decided the core of who I am is happiness, empathy, and love, which I've worked really hard to make my core because it didn't magically happen. I radiate out happiness, empathy, and love. I worked on me. I expect others that are close to me to also work on building their core character too.

The problem is that evil is often dressed up in beauty and eloquence. We must recognize the truth because it is simply true. Our hearts tell us the difference, so let's nurture the ability to be able to recognize the difference.

For those with evil words and vile acts, they need a clear message that their secrets will not be kept, their shadows will be put to light, and their lies will not be spread or accepted. We have each played a role in maintaining the societal mess we have now. We perpetuate the mess:

When we turn away and ignore it.

When we buy media that demeans others.

When we laugh at jokes that label others.

When we judge a victim.

When we protect an evil act with maintained secrets.

I am guilty of not talking enough of what path and what steps have brought me here. I'm changing that now.

Chapter 22

We Could All Talk More!

"Words are seeds that do more than blow around. They land in our hearts and not the ground. Be careful what you plant and careful what you say. You might have to eat what you planted one day." –Unknown

WHEN BAD THINGS HAPPEN, IT'S a positive coping skill to find other people who have gone through similar trials and emulate them. Socrates said there is nothing new under the sun. Every trial has happened before. It's unique because of our unique cumulative experiences, but something that happened to one human has happened to another human. Find someone who has coped well, and it will give you hope that you can rise above the pain to find the joy in life again.

When I was sixteen, a neighbor lady said, "You can make your life great." Her impressing upon me that my life could be something great gave me hope and strength. We as human beings can give each other strength. Which speaks to the third stage of abuse: advocacy.

I know it sounds so simple, so trite, so innocent, but it was the small kindnesses that saved me. It was these kinds of simple awareness that gave me hope and brought me to healing.

All too often we hear a story similar to this one: a teacher is trying to engrain the importance of sexual purity to his/her class of young adults. What the teacher doesn't know is that there is a young girl who has been molested or touched without her consent. This teacher uses an analogy. Maybe, "Who would want to use a tissue that has already been used?" or "Who chews already spit out gum?"

This is never okay, and I've lived all over and heard this in many different theologies. It isn't unique to any one religion. But, any Christian church can point to Christ. When a woman is caught in adultery and dragged before a crowd, the Savior doesn't say, "Well, you're disgusting, nobody wants a used tissue, and now the rest of your life will suck."

No. He says, "Neither do I condemn thee: go, and sin no more." (John 8:11)

If this is true with sin, how much more true is it when it is *not* a sin. No consent, no sin.

We are not defined by what happened to us. We are defined by what we are becoming. In every single religion there is a redeeming figure. In mine, we call that figure Jesus Christ. To say that you are a chewed-up piece of gum or a used tissue is an idea that comes from Satan.

In both religious and secular circles, our society has a problem with blaming the victim. And I think this goes back to the psychological reasons of trying to find ways to stop that from happening to us. But a lot of times teachers go with the route of trying to scare kids into not having sex too soon.

Shaming our children into obedience means they might do the right thing for the wrong reason. If we're open with our kids, we protect them not only from sexual assault—getting them away from dangerous situations or not going into dangerous situations—but we also can help them understand what line to not cross, and most importantly, what lines to not allow others to cross. We can also help raise them into sympathetic and kind adults. If they've always followed "Don't do that!" then when a friend does slip up, they might respond, "Well I didn't do that, why did she do that?"

Every experience has lessons in it; I share my story hoping to teach, in an appropriate way, options or tools and to offer hope to navigate the threats of evil in our society. Experience is a great teacher and so is sharing what we learn as others can learn from our experience. We teach and learn from others' experiences, so they hopefully don't have to have the same hardships. The next story is a difficult one to hear. It is included because of the witness of God's love, even in the grasp of unthinkable depravity, so I felt it needed to be shared.

Pedophile Ring

Evil exists. But when one knows great darkness, the opposite is available. Light not only equal but surpassing it. This next story comes from a friend that was introduced to me while I was writing this book. This survivor cannot go public. Why? Because her family was complicit in systematic abuse of not only her but many others, in a pedophile ring. We were put in contact and she has entrusted me with her story, and I hope the time will come that she can publicly share her story. Until then I carry this to you. The name of Yael has been chosen as a pseudonym, referencing a woman from the bible that stood up for herself. Read it. You'll chuckle at the parallel.

Throughout this book I have tried to be sensitive to the young readers that will hold these pages. **Please be warned that the following story may not be suitable for all audiences.**

Yael's Story

Yael grew up in a wealthy area, she was not an impoverished at-risk kid. Her friend that has known her since they were both young girls said they grew up in one of those nice neighborhoods that we think this kind of thing could never happen in.

Her mom would deliver her to a satanic cult for the weekend. Her brother would deliver her to a pedophile ring for money. Other family members knew, so she thought it was normal.

It is important to point out that this wasn't in another country, this was in California. A little three-year-old girl was taken, tied up and hidden away, not far from where other children were innocently enjoying a beach. It became normal for her to be abused because so many were abusing her, a trip to get an ice cream cone became a delivery to evil hands. On one such weekend trip with her mom to the cult, she and other young girls were chained up in a basement of a warehouse. In her own words: "Jesus was with me. He was telling me it wasn't my fault, her (referring to her mom) betrayal wasn't about me, and I was such a good little girl." Her captors would tell her that she had been bad, that her mom would report in on how the week at home had gone and they would twist that to control her and "punish" her. The immensity of manipulation and guilt poured onto this child just sickens me. The leader of this satanic cult was trained in military brainwashing tactics and used these skills on his young victims. As a child, Yael of course didn't understand this. As an adult she has been able to see him use his tactics and power to destroy those that have tried to out him.

Yael: "Even though I was scared and lonely, He was scared and lonely with me. I knew that Jesus loved me. I knew that He was my friend and we were in it together. The whole time I wondered what I had done wrong because they said I was so bad, they'd tell my mom."

I was given many pages of her journal to read. It is not easy reading. Yael was placed in evil's grasp by those that should have protected her, but her story is a testament that God is real. God has compensated Yael by giving her knowledge that God is real. She not only saw Jesus, but she also saw Satan.

Once during an assault, she had a vivid dream that she was back in a place she'd been before coming to this life. Her grandma was with her and other loved ones comforted her as her soul felt polluted by what was happening to her young body. In this dream, she felt concerned that her filthiness would somehow pollute her grandma. She told her grandma, "No one could ever love me. No mom. No grandma.

"My grandma told me she adored me and there was no one she was closer to in this whole world than me. Her mom, my great-grandma, kneeled down next to me and talked about how much she loved me and all the things she wanted to teach me about music. She said she'd been teaching me before I came to earth, but I hadn't had the chance to remember. I just couldn't comprehend their interest in me, but I knew they'd both trade places with me in a second and take the pain if they could.

"Then Jesus came and asked if He could hold me, but I was so embarrassed by how big and fat and dirty I was. I was going to make Him dirty, too. Grandma didn't hesitate, putting me in his arms even though I was gross. He told me that Satan himself had been trying to destroy me and hadn't, and that he wouldn't win. He wanted to show me who I was before I came to earth. I looked and saw that it was me following after Him and leaning down to help someone, just like He would do. I was so overwhelmed and overjoyed by seeing me. I loved myself and couldn't believe I was sweet, funny, kind, and a lot like Jesus. I was smart and bright, and I wanted to do what it would take to be like Him. I knew it would be hard, but I was convinced I could do it. I was so happy to see me before I came to earth. I was filled with love for myself, and awe.

"People had thrown yucky stuff on Jesus, too, but that didn't change His goodness or worth. He showed me that you could put up an invisible screen in front of yourself, but people didn't see it. They thought that it was hitting you, but really, it was just falling down the screen. I thought that was the best thing I'd ever seen! I giggled and laughed in front of the screen while stuff was being thrown at me, but it wasn't actually hitting me. I was actually really good at laughing before I came to earth. I had a gift for it, and I'd get it back.

"I knew I'd lose this ability to separate myself from what happened to me, but when I remembered, I'd have to choose to believe that I was a good girl. If I could choose to believe people loved me, and Jesus loved me, that's what would make all the bad stuff come off and how I'd heal.

"There was so much more. I love and adore Him, and I think my tears have already bathed His feet. I am so thankful for His tenderness, goodness, mercy, attentiveness, love, long suffering and his perpetual efforts to make Himself known to us. He is nothing but love and understanding, He just wants us with Him."

When I have heard stories of children that were hurt in unspeakable ways, I have always hoped and prayed that when evil choked the body's life away, that the soul of that child was somehow sheltered away from that scene. I like to think that the grace of God surrounds that child and holds him safe. This story of Jesus standing with Yael, sending her grandmother to support her, is a confirmation of my hope that they are not always alone with such evil.

One night, a sick, deranged man dressed up as Jesus then proceeded to rape Yael. It was so upsetting that her "brain shut down. That night, as I was playing with my toys, I felt the real Jesus there. I froze in terror. He held out His hand to me and said that the guy pretending to be Him put his hand over my mouth and I licked it to try to get it off my mouth, but it didn't have a hole in it. He told me His hands will always have a hole in it. He filled me with his love and I cried with him. I was four, I think. But I always relied on touching his hand and feeling the hole to make sure it was the right Jesus."

On another occasion, she was in a room where she and other children were being held in chains. "I saw Jesus sitting next to *each* of us. He came by my side, reassuring me that I had done nothing wrong. I saw Jesus go up to each one of the kids and reassure them that it wasn't their fault."

That one sentence echoes in my soul, doesn't that just sound like something Jesus would do? To comfort each one, each individually. I love this witness. I like to think that every child could see Jesus and hear His words. As Yael says, "Jesus was planning on following through, knowing his blood would be shed for us. However, when the time came to actually do it, he begged God to let the cup pass. It showed Jesus' humanity. He didn't like pain any more than the rest of us. He wished to avoid it, but he loved Heavenly Father more than He hated pain." When we think of the heavy, awful things that God knows about mankind, that He sees the things we humans are capable of doing to another, doesn't it bring strength to know the He has given a little girl a knowledge of His love? God is capable of bringing peace to her.

Yael shares, "I asked God, how do I go on? And I got the most delightful understanding. To the core of my soul, I felt that Jesus is my friend. He's been there with me. He's chosen to be there with me and He's chosen to stay. He won't leave me now. He adores me. We are in this together."

One day Yael was listening to the song "Amazing Grace" on repeat. "It struck me and I'm not sure why. A lot of my hurt is subconscious. But when I actually put words to my thoughts, they come out like this: I'm disgusting. I'm worthless. No one cares about me. I'm so gross. Why aren't I special? Why aren't I worth being loved and taken care of? I wish I were someone else. I wish I could be that person, then I'd be worthwhile.

"But thinking that I'm His, that I belong to Jesus...now, that's something. That attaches me to someone who is perfect. I also get constant reminders to be merciful to myself, and that this is not Heavenly Father doing this to me. And then I got it. Satan wants me to be quiet. Satan wants me to feel shame when I do speak. All my bad feelings are from Satan."

Yael has to fight the scars of what happened without the solace of saying openly this happened to protect her own safety and that of her children. I was happy to be told that her husband is a loving and tender man described as a "Godsend".

I am thankful for this story. Yael's experience tells me that Jesus does not delegate the comfort of the innocent; He Himself attends them.

Chapter 23

Your Cue to Set
the Stage of Your Life

THE DAY I POSTED MY thoughts on #metoo, the day I got a book offer, I cried a lot. Like walking through Kohl's for an exchange and tucking behind a rack of clothes to just cry a little more. Not because I had been molested, not because I hurt now. I cried because I realized that God expected me to do something about it. I cried because it felt too heavy a thing to not only dive into, but to walk through and try to explain to all who would read this why I was okay. Not only okay but thriving. My life is great. When I see the anger, when I see the messages sent to the victims and survivors of assault, rape, and molesting that they are now damaged, I know in my soul that idea is wrong. In fact it is evil to believe that any series of events defines our whole life.

That very same day, others' stories came pouring in from all over the world. It was shocking to read of the horrors that have happened here in my home state, my area with its tree lined streets. Yet even I was abused in a slice of perfect Americana. The truth is horrid, unthinkable acts of evil are happening every day in every country, province, state, city and town. Your town, too.

We want to look away. Here are the facts, according to www. dosomething.org: One in three girls, one in five boys will be molested, sexually abused before they turn 18. And those are just the reported cases. Human trafficking is a fancy word for slavery, and there are more people living in slavery today than at any other time in history. While my kids play innocently, I pray while your kids do too, children just like them are chained up and drugged so that despicable acts of sexual deviation can be fulfilled.

If we as a society condemn pedophilia, then we must not look away when we see it. We must reject it as acceptable. If we as a society condemn child molestations, then we must watch for signs and be a protector and an advocate for each and every victim. To root this out we cannot ever blame the survivor.

Part of the proceeds of this book go to Operation Underground Railroad, an organization that works to free those bound in sex slavery around the world, just like its namesake freed slaves from the South. If sharing the innermost painful stories of my past could help one child find hope to a great life, then the emotional diarrhea caused by writing it, the dark moments I went through, are more than worth it. I have had that compensation already in my life that what I experienced is worth it. In writing this book I have imagined you the reader. I have imagined what your pain is. I hope to have helped to give you the understanding that life can be, and will be, more than the pain you feel now. I hope that the tools taught here you will use, and above all I hope that you will feel the love and light of God in your life. I know what darkness you have been scarred by. But I know the light is not only equal to it but greater access to light and love can and will be yours.

What are we to do? What can be changed? I wish that I could tell you the straightforward, simple solution that would end the per-petration of sexual abuse and assault. I don't have that for you, I am sorry. The cause of this lies in the epic battle of right and wrong, light and dark. Each individual must decide where they stand in this battle. I hope that when you see innocence being stripped away, you will defend the victim. That when you feel trapped, you will push back and yell out "No." That you will put the full measure of the law upon those selfish and shallow enough to only think of their own sexual desires.

I hope that you will not buy media that glorifies rape or assault. When an artistic expression mocks, belittles, minimizes, or rationalizes ill treatment of another individual or group, that you will be repulsed by it and not fund it, not laugh, and not support it. Hate of any kind opens the door to abuse. It erodes safety boundaries, thus opening the door to worse offenses.

For those of you not touched by sexual violations through personal experience, you may want to look away; we did that as a society. We just told ourselves that it wasn't that big of a problem. Victims suffered in silence, survivors had boundaries that were not mended, and advocates like myself spoke quietly on the topic. Now, we are finding that our path forward is one of healing, hope, and advocacy. May the victims still in the grasp of abuse hear our message: we will protect you and we will nurture you. We know you will do great things in your life. You are not broken by evil, you are greater than that.

For the victim reading this or the person that wasn't safe still inside of you, it is my prayer that this book will help you see that you are capable of living an amazing life. *All the good* that life can offer will be yours, if you work for it. No one can give it to you, so now is your cue to set the stage of your life. I would like to think that this book has offered hope and a path to becoming an advocate.

I can't change what happened to Little Leta, but I have made her life awesome, and because of who I have become, it is my honor to write this book for you. I do this simply with the knowledge that one voice can change the life of another, and when you hear one voice, you will start to hear a choir of others cheering you on. I am thankful to be a woman I respect. Having love and respect for yourself is worth the self-work to get to this place of living a full and joyful life. It is a gift beyond price to get to share my life with a man who honors, respects and loves me.

My request of the world is this: when we talk about sexual abuse and assault, let us protect the victim, encourage the survivor, and champion the advocate. This is why words matter. Our negative words become ideas, and that turns into chains to hold us down. When we speak of #metoo, let us also speak of hope.

Last but not least, I credit my Savior Jesus Christ for tugging at my soul until I heard Him, pulling me from darkness. Everything I am mentally, physically, and spiritually, I can direct back to the love, grace and goodness from God. The Atonement of Jesus Christ is real; I invite you to test His promise of healing in your life.

Acknowledgements

THANK YOU TO SNOWY PEAKS Media for jumping on this project before I had time to really think about it or back down from what we both knew God expected me to do. Thank you for giving me complete control over content and believing in my vision for this book. Your faith in me show you're above profit, you really want to turn out content that helps the reader. Kirk Edwards, I'm glad I let you borrow my first book overnight, thank you for staying up late to find an unknown author and help my book get wider distribution.

Thank you to Heather Godfrey, my editor. The bond between an editor and writer is a partnership that those who haven't written a book may not understand. The bond between a writer and editor when the writer (me) has serious grammar issues is not an ideal editing job, and you handled it with so much grace, I think you like working with me! I feel like we've become sisters. I'm always going to tease you about giving you all my secrets and you put them in a book.

To the women that shared their experiences with me, both those that I quoted and those I couldn't name, I thank you for your courage in adding your voice to mine. The voices of hope as we combine our melody can overpower the voices of anger.

To my beta readers Pam Hepworth, Katie Holland, David Widdison, Sheryl Babcock, Cindy Woodruff, Vicki Tuaa and my hubby Nathan Greene. You were each chosen because of your ability to be honest to tell me the truth to help this book be the best it could be. We had a tight deadline and you met it. Thank you.

To my parents. It's a terrible thing to have your child hurt. You stood by me then. It is not easy to have a book written about how your friend betrayed you in the worst way. I recognize your pain and thank you for supporting this book, and for never once blaming me. Thank you.

Thank you to my brother Lance, my best friend as a kid. I'm still disturbed by spiders but I'm tough, just like you always said. Thank you for showing me the respect I should expect from men.

I am thankful to my husband, the best man I know, Nathan Greene. Your stalwart devotion to God attracted me to you, and continues to be your best trait. Marrying you was the best decision I ever made. Thank you for making many dinners because I was in the zone, and delivering dinner to me with a neck rub and words like, "I'm proud of you." I am stronger with you, I am braver and better with you. Thank you for being the man of my dreams and the keeper of my heart forever.

Thank you to my oldest son, Nathaniel, who is fifteen years old at the time of this writing. When I asked him, "Son, I've been offered a publishing contract to write a book on sexual abuse, how do you feel about your mom doing this?" He said, "Mom you have to do what God is asking you to do."

Thank you to my daughter Ailsa, who was thirteen at the time of writing. Her reply to my question was to clap and talk about her dear friend "Jaime" and other kids that have experienced the violation of sexual abuse. Her wish is that the book helps them.

Thank you to my daughter Katelynn who lives with God. I know you and your angel friends helped me find words to explain memories and feelings I haven't had to think about in a long time. I'm not putting off writing your book anymore.

To you the reader, I've imagined who you are, what your pain is. I've prayed to write the book you need. I think of the children, the child inside each of us. May we have the courage to talk to the children.

I have written this book for the girl or boy that cannot speak out, I was once that girl. It was a surprise to me that I should write this book, however it wasn't an accident. Unbeknownst to me, the groundwork was laid in my personality, choices, and career that called me to be a messenger of healing. I didn't see this coming, nor did I ask for this. The weakness of this book is of myself. I hope to not dilute the message. This is my manifesto of healing, to give hope to the victim, peace to the survivor, and to unite the advocates.

Lastly, I must recognize a loving God that spoke truth to me until I heard it. The grace and Atonement of Jesus Christ is real. I am a product of inviting Christ into my life.

Photo credit: Emily London

About the Author

L ETA GREENE IS LIVING THE life her younger self couldn't have imagined. As an image consultant and makeup artist since 1999, Leta has helped clients to not only look their best, but to feel their best. Leta has also built a multimillion dollar beauty business with SeneGence International, and is a sought after trainer for women entrepreneurs. Her message is one of honoring yourself through authenticity.

Leta has a thriving speaking career where she speaks on confidence and finding joy in life. She is a two-time TEDx speaker, and loves sharing the principles that make life amazing through her keynotes, workshops and speaking to youth. Some of the programs she offers are maturation programs for fifth grade girls, confidence workshops for tween and teen girls, joyful workshops for women, and seminars for parents on how to talk to your kids about sex. She is also an energetic keynote speaker for conferences and seminars on resiliency, personal responsibility and confidence. It is through humor, stories, and a new way of seeing the everyday that makes Leta's audiences of all ages want to hold on for more!

Her bestselling first book, *How to Embrace Your Inner Hotness,* outlines the steps to developing confidence and self-awareness. *Love Me Too,* a book she never planned on writing, is meant to share that life can be amazing even if one has experienced sexual abuse.

The greatest pride in her life is seeing the people her children are choosing to become. She lives in South Jordan, Utah, with her hubby, two kids and three cats.

CPSIA information can be obtained
at www.ICGtesting.com
Printed in the USA
FSHW02n0056031018
52569FS